Jessie Fioritto

Praying Your Way to Hope

A Devotional Journal

BARBOUR
PUBLISHING

Published by Barbour Publishing, Inc., 1810 Barbour Drive, Uhrichsville, Ohio 44683, www.barbourbooks.com

Our mission is to inspire the world with the life-changing message of the Bible.

 Member of the
Evangelical Christian
Publishers Association

Printed in China.

A GOOD FATHER

Give thanks to the LORD, for he is good. His love endures forever.
Give thanks to the God of gods. His love endures forever. Give thanks
to the Lord of lords: His love endures forever. To him who alone does
great wonders, His love endures forever. Who by his understanding
made the heavens, His love endures forever. Who spread out the
earth upon the waters, His love endures forever.
PSALM 136:1–6

Lord God of all creation, sometimes this world feels like it's imploding with chaos. It seems dark and dangerous and unpredictable. I question Your good intent and worry about a future that looks so uncertain. Thank You, God, for the reminder that You are good. No darkness can reside in Your unpolluted light. Your love endures forever, and You love me as Your own precious daughter. I belong to You, and You will shelter me and fill me with the bursting hope of an eternal future with You, my beloved Father. I may not always understand Your ways, because I know they are infinitely higher than mine, but I trust in Your love and goodwill toward Your child. In Jesus' name, amen.

Patient in Hope

We ourselves, who have the firstfruits of the Spirit, groan inwardly
as we wait eagerly for our adoption to sonship, the redemption of
our bodies. For in this hope we were saved. But hope that is seen is
no hope at all. Who hopes for what they already have? But if we
hope for what we do not yet have, we wait for it patiently.
In the same way, the Spirit helps us in our weakness.
ROMANS 8:23–26

Lord Jesus, thank You that this world is not all I have to look forward to. A fleeting life that ends in death is a bleak future indeed. But You've promised me an everlasting life in a redeemed body. And You've given me Your Holy Spirit as a depositon my future inheritance. I can endure the trials and pains of this world because my eyes are fixed on what is to come. Hope sustains me in this fallen place. And not only have You given me hope, but Your Holy Spirit lives in me as evidence of my salvation and helps me when I pray. I eagerly anticipate my coming life with You, when the weight of this world will fall away. Amen.

Joyful in Hope

Love must be sincere. Hate what is evil; cling to what is good.
Be devoted to one another in love. Honor one another above
yourselves. Never be lacking in zeal, but keep your spiritual fervor,
serving the Lord. Be joyful in hope, patient in affliction, faithful
in prayer. Share with the Lord's people who are in need. Practice
hospitality. Bless those who persecute you; bless and do not curse.
ROMANS 12:9–14

God, renew my joy. Keep it simmering inside me like a delicious, steaming soup on a cold and dismal day. I may not always feel happy about my circumstances, especially when storms come, but the hope that I have in You, Jesus, sustains my joy through difficult times. May others see it bubbling inside me and be drawn to its warmth. Lord, I'm ashamed that sometimes *zeal* and *fervor* aren't words that describe my attitude of service. Selfish desires derail me from my true kingdom-building purpose and promise me temporary comforts that are ultimately unsatisfying and empty. But I will cling to Your goodness, and through hope, Your Spirit's joy will once again quicken in my soul. In Jesus' precious name, amen.

Hope and a Future

"For I know the plans I have for you," declares the LORD, "plans to prosper you and not to harm you, plans to give you hope and a future. Then you will call on me and come and pray to me, and I will listen to you. You will seek me and find me when you seek me with all your heart. I will be found by you," declares the LORD.

JEREMIAH 29:11–14

. . . .

Father, it's too easy to ask why at times. Why is this happening to me, or why does anything bad have to happen ever if You are a God of love? But I know that questioning Your intent is a dangerous road for my soul to tread. You—the living Creator—always have a plan. You had a plan from the beginning of time. I choose to trust in Your good and loving designs for me. I have hope because You *didn't* just leave us here to flounder. Instead, You sent us Your Son, Jesus. He did for us what we couldn't accomplish in our own power—He died to wash away the stain of our sins so we could have a good future with You. Thank You for letting us find You. Amen.

Seeing Clearly

When I became a man, I put the ways of childhood behind me.
For now we see only a reflection as in a mirror; then we shall
see face to face. Now I know in part; then I shall know fully,
even as I am fully known. And now these three remain:
faith, hope and love. But the greatest of these is love.
1 Corinthians 13:11–13

Lord, I have gazed into antique mirrors. It's difficult to make out my features through the marred surface and dim reflection. I have to remind myself that this is also how I see You—through the limited lens of my humanity. I can just trace the outline of Your features but not quite see the fullness of Your glory. But I have the hope that one day I will see You face-to-face! I will know You as You so completely know every facet of who I am. For now I trust the shadow of You that I can see and the image of You that is etched in Your Word, but I also long for the day when I will know You more. In Jesus' name, amen.

NEVER ALONE

*"I took you from the ends of the earth, from its farthest corners
I called you. I said, 'You are my servant'; I have chosen you and
have not rejected you. So do not fear, for I am with you; do not be
dismayed, for I am your God. I will strengthen you and help
you; I will uphold you with my righteous right hand."*

ISAIAH 41:9–10

Heavenly Father, this life can be lonely and scary. Surrounded by an overcrowded world, I can still feel unseen and alone. But that isn't the truth. That lie comes from the enemy who would discourage and depress me with the illusion that I'm isolated and unlovable. But You, God, have a different message for me. One of hope. You say that I'm chosen. That I'm not rejected. That You will never leave me. I can walk in Your strength and with the promise of Your help. I am loved and cared for and seen. As You told Abraham's servant Hagar in the desert, You are the God who sees me. In Your presence, I am never alone. In the name of Jesus, amen.

My Only Hope

"Show me, LORD, my life's end and the number of my days;
let me know how fleeting my life is. You have made my days a
mere handbreadth; the span of my years is as nothing before you.
Everyone is but a breath, even those who seem secure. Surely
everyone goes around like a mere phantom; in vain they rush
about, heaping up wealth without knowing whose it will finally be.
But now, Lord, what do I look for? My hope is in you."

PSALM 39:4–7

Lord, I have tried to "find myself" in other things. I have trusted knowledge, money, and other people for my future. In my pride, I thought I could build my own fortress of security. I thought my footprint on this earth was bigger than it is. But You have shown me the futility in such thoughts. Money can't save me and people will fail me. My life here is less than a blink of Your eternal eye. I've learned that You are my only hope, God. Only You can save. Only You can give me a promising future that's so much better than anything I could ever hope to experience here. Praise You, Lord, that there's more than this fleeting existence. Amen.

DOOR OF HOPE

"But then I will win her back once again. I will lead her into the desert and speak tenderly to her there. I will return her vineyards to her and transform the Valley of Trouble into a gateway of hope. She will give herself to me there, as she did long ago when she was young, when I freed her from her captivity in Egypt."

HOSEA 2:14–15 NLT

. . . .

God, I have stumbled through deep hollows—shadowed and chilly places unreached by the sun. I have known trouble and hardship and heartbreak. Life hasn't always treated me with gentle hands. And I've run from You. But I cling to this promise: You can transform valleys of trouble into doors of hope. You came to bind up the brokenhearted and set captives free, Jesus. I have been a prisoner of my own despair, but no more! I'm leaving my chains and walking through the door of Your hope into freedom. You have wooed me with Your love, compassion, and faithfulness. I don't deserve Your attentiveness, Lord, but You've remained devoted to me in spite of my failures. In the beautiful name of Jesus, amen.

My Resting Place

*How long will you assault me? Would all of you throw me down—
this leaning wall, this tottering fence? Surely they intend to topple
me from my lofty place; they take delight in lies. With their mouths
they bless, but in their hearts they curse. Yes, my soul, find rest in
God; my hope comes from him. Truly he is my rock and my
salvation; he is my fortress, I will not be shaken.*

PSALM 62:3–6

Heavenly Father, at times I feel as if I'm surrounded by "frene-
mies." Why do we so harshly judge each other and take delight
in attacking one another's weaknesses? We may speak kindly, but
our hearts are overrun by jealousy and greed. God, navigating this
world is exhausting. But my weary soul has found a resting place
in You. I will not be shaken, because I have sunk my foundation
into Your bedrock. God, You are solid ground when others wash
out. The enemy may assault me, he may rattle my defenses looking
for vulnerabilities, but You are my fortress. Thank You, Jesus, for
bolstering my shaky walls and giving me a place of refuge. I can't
read Your Word without feeling hope. Amen.

My Anchor

So God has given both his promise and his oath. These two things are unchangeable because it is impossible for God to lie. Therefore, we who have fled to him for refuge can have great confidence as we hold to the hope that lies before us. This hope is a strong and trustworthy anchor for our souls. It leads us through the curtain into God's inner sanctuary. Jesus has already gone in there for us.

HEBREWS 6:18–20 NLT

God, You are the Promise Keeper and the Hope Giver. Your promises give flight to my hope, and it soars high on confident wings because I know that You can't lie. Everything You have said will happen just as You've planned. Just as Abraham patiently waited for his promised rewards, we will wait patiently, knowing that You keep Your promises to us. Instead of drifting on a sea of fear and uncertainty, I have moored myself to the anchor of hope in You. I can come directly to Your throne, God, because Jesus made it possible. And He intercedes for me. Even when I'm not sure what I need to pray, Your Holy Spirit has the words I lack. In the name of Your precious Son, Jesus, amen.

Sweet Wisdom

My child, eat honey, for it is good, and the honeycomb is sweet to the taste. In the same way, wisdom is sweet to your soul. If you find it, you will have a bright future, and your hopes will not be cut short.
PROVERBS 24:13–14 NLT

. . . .

Heavenly Father, the world markets its own brand of wisdom and understanding, and it can be persuasive and appear logical. But Your Word says that the fear of the Lord is the beginning of wisdom. Father, I want to honor You with my life and walk in wisdom as a daughter of the King. I want that bright and hope-filled future that You offer to all who are guided by Your wise counsel. My soul craves the truth of Your Word, and it delights my tongue like a decadent chocolate dessert dripping with warm fudge. Teach me to seek Your wisdom and direct my decisions, for I know my hopes will not be disappointed in You. In Jesus' name, amen.

The Light Has Come

*In the beginning was the Word, and the Word was with God,
and the Word was God. He was with God in the beginning.
Through him all things were made; without him nothing was
made that has been made. In him was life, and that life
was the light of all mankind. The light shines in the
darkness, and the darkness has not overcome it.*

John 1:1–5

Lord Jesus, how amazing that You have always been with God. In the beginning, You were the creative force who made all things. And not only did You make all things but You gave them life. Because You are the Life. This world can be so dark. Sin rules here, and Satan often seems to have the upper hand with his scheming traps. And those left in the dark too long lose hope. But You are the light, Jesus. You offer forgiveness and grace and life eternal. There's nothing more uplifting to someone lost in the gloom than glimpsing a bright porch light. Your light, which cannot be extinguished, shatters the darkness that threatens to overcome us. Amen.

Wings of Hope

The Lord. . .never grows weak or weary. No one can measure the depths of his understanding. He gives power to the weak and strength to the powerless. Even youths will become weak and tired, and young men will fall in exhaustion. But those who trust in the Lord will find new strength. They will soar high on wings like eagles. They will run and not grow weary. They will walk and not faint.
Isaiah 40:28–31 nlt

. . . .

Lord, I'm exhausted by the struggle of this world. I've been trying to do it all on my own. And I've been failing miserably. I'm driven to my knees by weakness. I was about to collapse in hopeless despair—but then I looked up to heaven and I found You. The tireless Creator. The Strength Giver. Lord God, I trust You. I trust Your understanding of every impossible and strength-sapping situation I'll ever encounter, and I give them to You. I'm offloading my stress onto the wide span of Your strong shoulders. I can do nothing without You. Pour new strength into my weary body. I want to soar like the eagles and work in Your kingdom zealously. In Jesus' name, amen.

HOPE IN FAILURE

The thought of my suffering and homelessness is bitter beyond words. I will never forget this awful time, as I grieve over my loss. Yet I still dare to hope when I remember this: The faithful love of the LORD never ends! His mercies never cease. Great is his faithfulness; his mercies begin afresh each morning. I say to myself, "The LORD is my inheritance; therefore, I will hope in him!"

LAMENTATIONS 3:19–24 NLT

Heavenly Father, sometimes our hopes are dashed in this world. Things don't turn out the way we had planned and we watch our desires slip from our grasp. We lose things. We lose people. Sometimes we just lose. But Your Word kindles hope in my soul. Your faithful love has no end. Every morning I can begin again with a fresh helping of Your mercy. I may not achieve greatness or success in this world, but You are my inheritance. I am a daughter with a royal endowment waiting for me. I *do* have a sparkling future to look forward to—with You. Keep my heart from bitterness, Lord, when happiness flees and suffering resides with me. I will grip tightly to my hope in You. Amen.

PRAISE INTO HOPE

I will go to the altar of God, to God, my joy and my delight.
I will praise you with the lyre, O God, my God. Why, my soul,
are you downcast? Why so disturbed within me? Put your
hope in God, for I will yet praise him, my Savior and my God.
PSALM 43:4–5

God, why do my worries overcome me? Why do I give in to depression and anxiety? Instead of allowing such destructive thoughts to run me into the ground, I need to come to You. I need to praise all of Your amazing attributes. When my focus remains on Your greatness, Lord, I'm not overwhelmed by my problems. I can see more clearly how capable You are of handling every issue. I begin to understand how silly I am to despair when the God of all creation is in charge. Lord, You are great and majestic, powerful and wise. I love You because You first cast Your love upon me, unworthy as I am. You chose me and saved me. Thank You, Jesus. Amen.

DELIGHTED TO KNOW ME

The LORD, the King of Israel, is with you; never again will you fear any harm. On that day they will say to Jerusalem, "Do not fear, Zion; do not let your hands hang limp. The LORD your God is with you, the Mighty Warrior who saves. He will take great delight in you; in his love he will no longer rebuke you, but will rejoice over you with singing."
ZEPHANIAH 3:15–17

. . . .

Lord, I feel disliked and unaccepted. Does anyone cherish my friendship or the person that You made me to be? The enemy tells me I'm overlooked and unappreciated by everyone. But, Father, Your Word says something different. It tells me something bright and encouraging. Even if every person on this earth is ambivalent to my presence here, You take great delight in me. You cherish me and rejoice over me. You're so happy to see me that You sing with joy when I enter Your courts. Because You formed every cell of my being and molded every facet of my personality, You think I'm the best thing You've ever done! Thank You for loving me. In the name of Your Son, Jesus, amen.

All I Need

The LORD is my shepherd; I have all that I need. He lets me rest in green meadows; he leads me beside peaceful streams. He renews my strength. He guides me along right paths, bringing honor to his name. Even when I walk through the darkest valley, I will not be afraid, for you are close beside me. Your rod and your staff protect and comfort me.
PSALM 23:1–4 NLT

God, we're so unsatisfied and greedy. More stuff, bigger houses, better-paying jobs, luxurious vacations—we just want more. It's all too tempting to get whirled up into the cyclone of more. I think, *If I just made a few hundred dollars more every month, I'd be happy. If my house was remodeled, I'd be happy.* But would I? This hungry beast is never satisfied and leaves a wake of torn-up lives and brokenness behind. Father, instead of insatiable desires, You offer me contentment and rest. In You my every need is met. I realize that I have been seeking fulfillment but pursuing emptiness. But I've found the Shepherd of my soul. Thank You, God, that You are all I've ever needed. Amen.

INTERCESSOR

The Holy Spirit prays for us with groanings that cannot be expressed in words. And the Father who knows all hearts knows what the Spirit is saying, for the Spirit pleads for us believers in harmony with God's own will. And we know that God causes everything to work together for the good of those who love God and are called according to his purpose for them.
ROMANS 8:26–28 NLT

Lord, I don't pretend to understand Your will in every situation. Often I don't even know which outcome to pray for. I know what I want in the moment, but I'm blinded by my shortsightedness. It's a great relief to know that You see the endgame, and You've given me Your Holy Spirit to pray for me when I have no words. You work every circumstance for the good of Your kingdom and Your children who love You. I may suffer here, but You don't waste a single moment of my life. Instead, You use them to make me more like Jesus. Thank You for refining me into a useful instrument. Smooth away my ragged edges so I can be used by You. Amen.

I BELIEVE

It was not with perishable things such as silver or gold that you were redeemed from the empty way of life handed down to you from your ancestors, but with the precious blood of Christ, a lamb without blemish or defect. He was chosen before the creation of the world, but was revealed in these last times for your sake. Through him you believe in God, who raised him from the dead and glorified him, and so your faith and hope are in God.

I PETER 1:18–21

God, I believe in You. I believe in Your love for me. And I believe that You sent Jesus to die for me. How awesome is Your love and wisdom, Father, that You chose Him for this purpose before You even spoke the first word of creation. I believe that You raised Him from the dead and that He is preparing my forever home with You for the day I will join You in eternity. My hope lives strong because I believe every word You have spoken. I experience Your love for me in the countless ways You provide for me, and I see it in Your exquisite care for my eternal soul. You didn't have to die, but You did. For me. Thank You, Jesus. Amen.

New Hope

So each generation should set its hope anew on God, not forgetting
his glorious miracles and obeying his commands. Then they will not
be like their ancestors—stubborn, rebellious, and unfaithful,
refusing to give their hearts to God.
PSALM 78:7–8 NLT

Lord of creation, I am in awe of the magnificent things You have done. Limitless—Your power, might, and wisdom are without border. My mind strains to understand exactly who You are. I know that I will never achieve a full knowledge of You here in this place, but I long to know more. You have done the most amazing things and set the most intricate plan into play for this world. Father, keep me from the mistakes of those who have gone before me. I give You my heart, my soul, my body, and my mind. Cleanse me of my stubbornness and unfaithful inclinations so I can follow You in obedience and love. You offer fresh hope for each generation. In Jesus' name, amen.

THE NEW ME

And he died for all, that those who live should no longer live for themselves but for him who died for them and was raised again. So from now on we regard no one from a worldly point of view. Though we once regarded Christ in this way, we do so no longer. Therefore, if anyone is in Christ, the new creation has come: The old has gone, the new is here!
2 CORINTHIANS 5:15–17

God, I thought there was no hope for me to ever be anything different. I thought I could never climb out of the deep sludge that filled the rut I was living in. I was convinced I wasn't worth much. The world surely didn't see even a glimmer of potential in me. But You did. You saw me as precious. You lifted me out by a nail-marked hand and made me into something new. Praise You, Jesus, the old, haggard me is gone. I'm different and better. It's me 2.0! Now I'm truly alive, and I spend my days living for You because You died but live again. I was dead too—dead in my sin and hopelessness—but no longer. In the saving name of Jesus, amen.

Bigger Plans

"You will conceive and give birth to a son, and you are to call him Jesus. He will be great and will be called the Son of the Most High. The Lord God will give him the throne of his father David, and he will reign over Jacob's descendants forever; his kingdom will never end."
LUKE 1:31–33

Lord, Your plans are always far greater than anything I could imagine with my limited mental faculties. The Jewish people expected Your prophecies to be fulfilled by a mighty and powerful earthly king. They wanted a military and political victory over their oppressors. But instead You sent a baby born in a barn and heralded His coming to poor, outcast shepherds. And yet you gave us so much more than a king—You gave us a Savior. You gave us hope and love and relationship with You. You gave us mercy and grace and an everlasting kingdom that's not of this world. You gave us Jesus. Father, teach me to trust Your plans because the nuances of Your design are fantastically beyond my wildest dreams. In Jesus' name, amen.

Borrowed Righteousness

But we who live by the Spirit eagerly wait to receive by faith the righteousness God has promised to us. For when we place our faith in Christ Jesus, there is no benefit in being circumcised or being uncircumcised. What is important is faith expressing itself in love.

GALATIANS 5:5–6 NLT

God, I'm not good enough by myself. I'm unworthy, and I mess up more than I care to admit. And that's okay. Because I praise You, Jesus, that no amount of rule-following can make me truly righteous. I can't earn Your love through my actions and good deeds, because You've already given it freely to me. I am made clean in Your eyes only through faith and the cleansing blood of Jesus. And while there's nothing wrong with doing good works for Your kingdom, what You require of Your followers is love. Lord, help me love better. My capacity for love often seems so limited compared to the unfathomable depth of Yours. Teach me to live in the Spirit and produce His fruits. Amen.

A God Who Answers

*Those who would harm me talk of my ruin; all day long they scheme and lie. I am like the deaf, who cannot hear, like the mute, who cannot speak; I have become like one who does not hear, whose mouth can offer no reply. L*ORD*, I wait for you; you will answer, Lord my God.*

PSALM 38:12–15

Heavenly Father, I plead to You in prayer day after day and sometimes it seems the heavens echo back with deafening silence. I'm tempted to wonder if You're listening, if You care. But then I find promises in Your Word that sprout new hope in my heart like spring flowers unfurling their faces to the sun. You are a God who hears and answers. Maybe not on my time line or within my plans, but You do answer. Give me patience, Lord. So many before me have blundered badly when their patience failed and they rushed in to "help" Your plans along. I will wait for You, Father, because I trust that You are even now working out the answers. In the name of Jesus, amen.

Enlighten Me

I keep asking that the God of our Lord Jesus Christ, the glorious Father, may give you the Spirit of wisdom and revelation, so that you may know him better. I pray that the eyes of your heart may be enlightened in order that you may know the hope to which he has called you, the riches of his glorious inheritance in his holy people, and his incomparably great power for us who believe.

Ephesians 1:17–19

. . . .

Lord, open the eyes of my heart. I want to know You with my whole being, not just have head knowledge of You. Send Your Spirit of wisdom and revelation to me so I can learn more about You and experience Your ways. Father, You haven't called me to a drab existence. You called me into hope! Reveal Yourself to me in new ways today. When I'm tempted to feel discouraged because others seem to be sailing blissfully along toward their happy earthly goals while I struggle and stumble after You, remind me of my future. I have a rich inheritance as Your daughter. And though I may be weak, You are not. Your incomparable power backs me. In the name of Your Son, Jesus, amen.

UNDAUNTED

Therefore we do not lose heart. Though outwardly we are wasting away, yet inwardly we are being renewed day by day. For our light and momentary troubles are achieving for us an eternal glory that far outweighs them all. So we fix our eyes not on what is seen, but on what is unseen, since what is seen is temporary, but what is unseen is eternal.

2 CORINTHIANS 4:16–18

God, our perspective has a way of carving us like a sculptor's chisel. I'm often tempted to fixate on my problems, failures, and hardships. Compared to the comfort and ease of some in this world, the believer's journey can seem rigorous and far too challenging. When I focus on here and now, discouragement edges into my thoughts because I can't see with my eyes the kingdom I'm waiting for. But, Lord, You call this life light and momentary trouble—a passing discomfort that will earn me eternal glory! Instead of straying to the temporary, may my mind be locked on the eternal. Then I will live for You, undaunted by my earthly circumstances, and my soul will be renewed. In Jesus' name, amen.

Hope in Loss

Brothers and sisters, we do not want you to be uninformed about those who sleep in death, so that you do not grieve like the rest of mankind, who have no hope. For we believe that Jesus died and rose again, and so we believe that God will bring with Jesus those who have fallen asleep in him.

1 Thessalonians 4:13–14

Heavenly Father, I'm grieving right now. I've lost someone I loved and their absence has gouged a rift in me. I will walk out the remainder of my days here without them, and that will be hard and painful sometimes. But praise You, Lord, I am not without hope, for my loved one is with You. You are Lord even over death. You died on the cross but were resurrected on the third day. Jesus, You are alive! And I know that because You live, one day I will be reunited with those whom I love. For every believer who loves You, Jesus, death is the doorway to the glory of Your eternity. Amen.

No Condemnation

Therefore, there is now no condemnation for those who are in Christ Jesus, because through Christ Jesus the law of the Spirit who gives life has set you free from the law of sin and death. For what the law was powerless to do because it was weakened by the flesh, God did by sending his own Son in the likeness of sinful flesh to be a sin offering.

ROMANS 8:1–3

. . . .

Lord, voices of shame shout at me inside my head. They remind me of all the wrong things I've ever done and tell me I will never be good enough. I'm guilty of so many things, and I know it. I know that, just like the woman caught in adultery and dragged before You, Jesus, I've earned the wages of my sins—death. But You have silenced those voices for all eternity! You set me free by becoming my sin offering and establishing the law of the Spirit who gives life. Life instead of death! No, I will never be worthy, but I don't have to be. Praise You, Jesus, I need only abide in You and I am no longer condemned. Amen.

The Spirit of Understanding

The Spirit searches all things, even the deep things of God. For who knows a person's thoughts except their own spirit within them? In the same way no one knows the thoughts of God except the Spirit of God. What we have received is not the spirit of the world, but the Spirit who is from God, so that we may understand what God has freely given us.

1 Corinthians 2:10–12

. . . .

God, the world thinks it owns wisdom and understanding, but I know that true understanding of this world and our ultimate destiny comes from You. You authored life, Father. And Your Spirit knows Your thoughts. When I committed my life to You, I received Your Spirit to be my instructor. Show me the deep mysteries of Your ways, Lord. Give me greater understanding of the precious gift You bestowed on me. Because You live in me I can understand spiritual truths that baffle those who don't know You. The world is confused by You, Lord, because Your ways don't conform to contemporary "wisdom." Thank You for giving me understanding, and help me bring others to You. Amen.

PEACE FOREVER

*Of the greatness of his government and peace there will be no end.
He will reign on David's throne and over his kingdom, establishing
and upholding it with justice and righteousness from that time on and
forever. The zeal of the* Lord *Almighty will accomplish this.*

ISAIAH 9:7

Father, peace—we all want to live in it, but it seems our lives here
are held in the iron grip of calamity. Wars erupt all over the world,
and Your followers are increasingly persecuted and criticized. But
this shouldn't surprise me. You said to remember that the world
hated You before it hated me. And You have promised us a better kingdom, a place where the greatness of Your government and
peace will have no end. My mind thrills at the thought of a world
swathed in peace. No fighting. No killing. No arguing. No jealousy
and gossip and petty backbiting. Harmony will reign supreme.
Lord, I long to dwell in this place with You. In Jesus' name, amen.

HOPE IN SUFFERING

Through whom we have gained access by faith into this grace in which we now stand. And we boast in the hope of the glory of God. Not only so, but we also glory in our sufferings, because we know that suffering produces perseverance; perseverance, character; and character, hope. And hope does not put us to shame, because God's love has been poured out into our hearts through the Holy Spirit, who has been given to us.

ROMANS 5:2–5

. . . .

Lord, I'm no different than anyone else. I don't like to suffer. I enjoy my comfort, and I don't want to go through difficult circumstances. But I know that even in my pain Your glory is being achieved. Through my pain, You are still working, and You are still in control of the universe. You promised that You would work everything for my good if I love You. And You do. Through my trials, You refine me into a person of perseverance, character, and hope. My hope in You will never disappoint me. You've filled my heart with Your love and given me Your Holy Spirit. I stand in grace because of Jesus. My struggles here have purpose in Your kingdom. In Jesus' name, amen.

GOD OF HOPE

Isaiah says, "The Root of Jesse will spring up, one who will arise to rule over the nations; in him the Gentiles will hope." May the God of hope fill you with all joy and peace as you trust in him, so that you may overflow with hope by the power of the Holy Spirit.

ROMANS 15:12–13

. . . .

God, without You, this world would seem unpredictable and unsafe. Without You, it would be so easy to think life is pointless. We live a short life, get what we can, and die. What hope is there without a greater purpose and calling than ourselves? But You, God, put meaning into my existence. You have a plan. You created us to love You and have been working out Your purpose in generation after generation. Because of You I have an internal calm in a confusing world. My heart is filled with joy and peace because I trust You. I trust Your plan, and I trust that You have a future for me. Thank You for giving me peace, hope, and joy. In the precious name of Jesus, amen.

CONFIDENT HOPE

*Faith shows the reality of what we hope for; it is the evidence
of things we cannot see. Through their faith, the people
in days of old earned a good reputation.*

HEBREWS 11:1–2 NLT

Heavenly Father, I praise Your name that there's no such thing
as blind faith in You. You haven't left me with no assurance that
what You've promised will come true. Instead, You've shown me
Your stellar record of thousands of years of promise keeping in
the Bible. How could I not trust that kind of integrity? You do and
have always done what You say You will do. I have confidence that
what I hope for is real. Eternity with You is real. You are really
there for me, God. You've given me evidence of the things I can't
see through my faith in You. My doubts have fled in the face of
overwhelming evidence that You exist. In Jesus' holy name, amen.

Praise Him

As for me, I will always have hope; I will praise you more and more. My mouth will tell of your righteous deeds, of your saving acts all day long—though I know not how to relate them all.

PSALM 71:14–15

. . . .

Lord, praising You is the best cure for depression and despair. I often become enmeshed in my own problems and all that is wrong in the world and forget how great You are. But today I choose praise over melancholy. Because as the Psalmist wrote, "I will always have hope." God, I am saved. I am redeemed. I am chosen. I am forgiven. You love me so much that You gave Your life in ransom for mine and are even now preparing a beautiful home for me in eternity. I don't deserve any of this! In fact, what I deserve is punishment, but You've given me grace instead. And on top of Your mercy, You've poured good gifts upon me. Praise You, Jesus. Amen.

MY SALVATION

The LORD is good to those whose hope is in him, to the one who seeks him; it is good to wait quietly for the salvation of the LORD.
LAMENTATIONS 3:25–26

. . . .

Lord, Your goodness flows to those who depend on You and search for You. In my stubbornness, I try to do things my own way and believe I can be self-reliant. I quote Your Word as "I can do all things" and too often conveniently forget the "through Christ who strengthens me" part. I think that I should be my own answer and create all my own solutions. And when the plates I'm spinning shatter at my feet, I remember to seek You. Lord, You are my answer and the solution to every problem. Help me to seek You more and trust that You have everything in hand. Any control I think I have is an illusion anyway. So I wait for You. In Jesus' name, amen.

He Is Light

*This is the message we have heard from him and declare to you:
God is light; in him there is no darkness at all. If we claim to have
fellowship with him and yet walk in the darkness, we lie and do not
live out the truth. But if we walk in the light, as he is in the light,
we have fellowship with one another, and the blood of
Jesus, his Son, purifies us from all sin.*

1 John 1:5–7

Heavenly Father, sometimes I forget who You are and apply human standards to Your character. But Your Word promises that You are light and only light. Nothing dark can coexist with You. This news is so wonderful because it means that I can trust You fully. You have no selfish or evil ulterior motives for anything that You do. Everything You say is truth. I can have a relationship with You, my Friend, the One who has robed me in borrowed righteousness and forgiven every wrong deed I've ever committed. Strengthen me to walk in Your light. My sinful nature is tempted by the darkness, but I want to keep to the light, Father! In Jesus' name, amen.

HE IS TRUSTWORTHY

God is not human, that he should lie, not a human being,
that he should change his mind. Does he speak and
then not act? Does he promise and not fulfill?

NUMBERS 23:19

Lord God, I know that my hope for an amazing eternity with You is real because You are trustworthy. You never change Your mind, and You aren't capable of lies. Throughout the ages, Your promises have always been upheld. Because of this, I know that my hope of walking the streets of gold in heaven will not be disappointed. You have promised those who love You a beautiful home where sin and death no longer exist, where the light of Your glory shines so brightly that the sun is obsolete, and where we can worship at Your throne. You have unimaginable good things in store for Your children. Here, I'm but a stranger passing through. I long for my true home with You. Amen.

LIVING WATER

Jesus answered, "Everyone who drinks this water will be thirsty again, but whoever drinks the water I give them will never thirst. Indeed, the water I give them will become in them a spring of water welling up to eternal life."
JOHN 4:13–14

Jesus, You gave this woman at the well such hope. She was searching for fulfillment and dying of thirst for something greater, much like all of us today. To never thirst again for acceptance. To never thirst again for forgiveness. To never thirst again for love. To have a life of eternity. You have quenched these needs and so many others, Jesus. You are the living water. I can drink of Your message and go away satisfied. I will never thirst for anything else now that I have known You. I can no longer seek meaning in houses or money or any of the empty idols I have chased. Knowing You has unveiled the true reality of my existence. In Jesus' name, amen.

Hope of Glory

Since, then, you have been raised with Christ, set your hearts on things above, where Christ is, seated at the right hand of God. Set your minds on things above, not on earthly things. For you died, and your life is now hidden with Christ in God. When Christ, who is your life, appears, then you also will appear with him in glory.

Colossians 3:1–4

. . . .

Father, C. S. Lewis described our human condition well: "Most people, if they had really learned to look into their own hearts, would know that they do want, and want acutely, something that cannot be had in this world. There are all sorts of things in this world that offer to give it to you, but they never quite keep their promise."[1] "At present we are on. . .the wrong side of the door. We discern the freshness and purity of morning, but they do not make us fresh and pure. We cannot mingle with the splendours we see. But all the leaves of the New Testament are rustling with the rumour that it will not always be so. Some day, God willing, we shall get in. . .put on its glory."[2] Amen.

....

....

....

....

....

....

....

....

....

1 C. S. Lewis, *The Complete C. S. Lewis Signature Classics* (New York: Harper San Francisco, 2002), 113.
2 C. S. Lewis, *The Weight of Glory* (New York: HarperCollins, 1980), 43.

Overcomers

In fact, this is love for God: to keep his commands. And his commands are not burdensome, for everyone born of God overcomes the world. This is the victory that has overcome the world, even our faith. Who is it that overcomes the world? Only the one who believes that Jesus is the Son of God.

1 John 5:3–5

. . . .

God, my desire is to grow in my faith to be like Jesus. I want to do the things You say I should and avoid the sins that would entangle me and hinder my ability to fulfill Your plans for me. Sometimes I fall and mess up in big ways, like Peter who denied You, Jesus. But still there's hope for me. Instead of shame for my failures, I return to You and receive Your grace just as Peter did on that beach by the lake after Your resurrection. You have won the victory already, and You have made me into an overcomer. I can overcome this world of sin because I believe that You, Jesus, are the Son of the most high God. Amen.

SEEK AND FIND

"Ask and it will be given to you; seek and you will find; knock and the door will be opened to you. For everyone who asks receives; the one who seeks finds; and to the one who knocks, the door will be opened."
MATTHEW 7:7–8

Lord, You don't make Yourself elusive to us. You don't hide and evade our searching hearts. Instead, You promise that if we seek we will find. You will open the door and introduce Yourself to any stranger who knocks. God, how astonishing to realize that a small, seemingly insignificant speck of Your creation like me can know and have a relationship with the eternal God of the universe. I'm humbled that You would answer my probing knocks and invite me in to know You better. You want me to know You deeply and fully and to experience the fathomless depth of Your pure love for me. You desire a genuine relationship. Thank You, God, for the honor of calling You Friend. In Jesus' name, amen.

THE PROMISE OF PARADISE

*One of the criminals who hung there hurled insults at him. . . . But the
other criminal rebuked him. "Don't you fear God," he said, "since you
are under the same sentence? We are punished justly, for we are getting
what our deeds deserve. But this man has done nothing wrong."
Then he said, "Jesus, remember me when you come into your
kingdom." Jesus answered him, "Truly I tell you,
today you will be with me in paradise."*

LUKE 23:39–43

Father, beside Your innocent Son hung two criminals on crosses
just like His. Two men who had lived sinful, evil lives. One of them
entered paradise with You and one did not. By his own admission,
they deserved their punishment. But the only thing that mattered
at the gates of paradise was not an impressive résumé of goodness
but rather his belief in You as the Lamb who takes away the sins of
the world. Thank You, Jesus, that You took God's wrath and my
punishment upon Yourself. Thank You that I don't have to be good
enough, because I can't be. I've earned my punishment just like
those two men who died with You, but You gave me life instead of
death, paradise instead of punishment. Amen.

ABUNDANT LIFE

"I am the gate for the sheep. All who have come before me are thieves and robbers, but the sheep have not listened to them. I am the gate; whoever enters through me will be saved. They will come in and go out, and find pasture. The thief comes only to steal and kill and destroy; I have come that they may have life, and have it to the full."

JOHN 10:7–10

. . . .

Lord, You are the true Gatekeeper. Satan circulates many false messages through his lies, but You are the Way and the Truth. Satan's agenda is to steal and kill and destroy—to abandon us to hopelessness. He would lead us away from You and enslave us with his false promises, but You came to give us a full life. You don't promise possessions or fame or power here on earth. No, what You offer is so much better. You offer me an awesome spiritual life that will last forever. I am alive in You, Jesus, and it is deep and quenching and free. It's far more amazing than anything I could ever imagine. In Jesus' name, amen.

Shouts of Joy

He will yet fill your mouth with laughter
and your lips with shouts of joy.
Job 8:21

Loving Father in heaven, thank You for blessing me with the gifts of laughter and hope. You haven't called me to an existence of joyless solemnity, but instead You came to give life—a full and everlasting life of hope in You. Sometimes I allow my difficulties and pain to rob me of the hope that lives within me. But no longer! I rejoice in You always, because the goodness You have waiting for me in heaven is unimaginable to my fragile human mind. You have given me a new spiritual life right now that spills over to a dark world filled with others who are searching for peace and hope that is found only in You. In the name of Jesus, amen.

CONFIDENT

But let us who live in the light be clearheaded, protected by the armor of faith and love, and wearing as our helmet the confidence of our salvation. For God chose to save us through our Lord Jesus Christ, not to pour out his anger on us. Christ died for us so that, whether we are dead or alive when he returns, we can live with him forever.

1 THESSALONIANS 5:8–10 NLT

God, I'm so grateful that I can be confident in my salvation. You gave us clear and concise instructions on what we must do to be saved—nothing except believe and confess. I don't have to wonder if the scale weighing my deeds will tip in favor of goodness, because You did it all, Jesus. I will live forever with You because Your blood covers my sin. The enemy may try to convince me that what I've done has crossed the limits of Your grace, but I know the truth of Your infinite mercy. I am sure of my salvation through Jesus and that confidence conquers all doubt and protects me from Satan's deadly arrows. I am Yours, now and forever. Amen.

Made New

Therefore, if anyone is in Christ, the new creation has come: The old has gone, the new is here! All this is from God, who reconciled us to himself through Christ and gave us the ministry of reconciliation: that God was reconciling the world to himself in Christ, not counting people's sins against them. And he has committed to us the message of reconciliation.

2 Corinthians 5:17–19

God, I'm broken. I live in a broken world. I'm enmeshed in an existence filled with war and hatred, messed-up families, selfishness, and abuse. I've tried to fix the brokenness in my life. I've run after success and relationships, but I can't mend what's wrong by using the things of this world. I can't mend the sin in my life. But You can, Jesus. God, all I have to do is surrender to You and repent. You came and died so that I could be regenerated into something new in Christ. You have a plan of redemption for this world, Father. I'm not broken anymore! I have been remade in Jesus. Reconciled to God. I am new! In Jesus' name, amen.

LOVED

There is no fear in love. But perfect love drives out fear, because fear has to do with punishment. The one who fears is not made perfect in love. We love because he first loved us.

1 JOHN 4:18–19

Father, You loved me first. I can't work my way into Your affections. And I don't have to! You have always loved me. You loved me so fully that Your Son took the punishment that was meant for me. Your perfect love drives away all my fears. You loved me even though I am a sinner. I will never be perfect on this earth. But I am forgiven. When You look at me, You no longer see the ragged, dirty shreds of sin I was garbed in. Now, You see the pristine, shining righteousness of Your Son. Father, fill me with Your love and allow it to overflow the borders of my life onto everyone I meet. In the name of Jesus, amen.

HE IS GOD

He says, "Be still, and know that I am God; I will be exalted
among the nations, I will be exalted in the earth." The LORD
Almighty is with us; the God of Jacob is our fortress.
PSALM 46:10–11

Lord, You are God and I am not. That realization brings me peace and hope and security. I don't have to attempt to control the universe. I can simply be still and recognize Your ultimate power and authority. I trust You, loving Father, to attend to the details of my life. I can't pretend to understand the intricacies of Your plans. Indeed, who am I to question them? But I can rest in my knowledge of Your good character. The weight of chasing my destiny and forging my path has been lifted since I put my trust in You. You are all-powerful and limitless in all Your ways. You are my God. In Jesus' name, amen.

A WAY THROUGH TEMPTATION

No temptation has overtaken you except what is common to mankind.
And God is faithful; he will not let you be tempted beyond what
you can bear. But when you are tempted, he will also
provide a way out so that you can endure it.
1 CORINTHIANS 10:13

Lord, enticing sins abound in this world. It can be so easy to lose my focus on You and allow myself to fall into sin. The enemy spreads his lies freely in this world, testing my will and my devotion to You. I can relate to the apostle Paul who said that the things he wanted to do he did not do and the things he hated he did. Sinning can feel like eating that death-by-chocolate cupcake (or several) while I'm dieting. My mind knows it's unhealthy for my body, but the pleasure of tasting it overwhelms my will. But You are faithful, God. If I turn to You, You've promised to help me endure. Strengthen me to stand. In Jesus' name, amen.

FREEDOM

*It is for freedom that Christ has set us free. Stand firm, then,
and do not let yourselves be burdened again by a yoke of slavery.*
GALATIANS 5:1

Jesus, You have set me free! I feel renewed and refreshed since I've started living my life for You. Before, I lived for myself and fulfilling all my selfish wants. I thought I was free in the belief that I could do whatever made me happy, but I felt so empty. And truly I wasn't free at all. I was bound in the chains of sin, controlled by my desire. I was living in a gilded prison of my own making. But You showed me a different way, Jesus! Now I am truly free. Free from a load of guilt and satisfied by Your living water. Following You is my new purpose. Becoming a slave to righteousness has set me free. In the name of Jesus, amen.

He Guides Me

Trust in the LORD with all your heart and lean not on your own understanding; in all your ways submit to him, and he will make your paths straight.

PROVERBS 3:5–6

Father, making decisions can be so confusing. Sometimes I don't know which way to turn. Navigating the fog of this world disorients me. Thank You for always being my guidance system. I trust You and Your Word above my own feeble attempts to understand all the threads You are weaving together in Your master plan. Jesus, I submit my life to You. And because I have laid all my decisions before You and asked for Your wisdom, I know that You will steady my course. I won't run aground in the murky waters of this life, because You are my lighthouse. You are the blazing beacon that guides me through the darkness into right choices. In Your name, Jesus, amen.

A Better Hope

For the law never made anything perfect. But now we have confidence
in a better hope, through which we draw near to God.
HEBREWS 7:19 NLT

. . . .

Heavenly Father, thank You for sending Jesus to provide us with
a better hope of being close to You. You knew that the Law would
not save us fallible humans. We can't help but mess up and break
the rules, sometimes a lot. Failure seems to be our default setting,
and no matter how hard we try, our efforts to achieve righteousness through the Law are feeble and steeped in failure. But then
You sent us Jesus and rent the curtain that prevented our entry
into Your inner sanctuary. Now we have a better way to draw near
to You. Instead of following rules, we can have a personal relationship with You, Father. We can know You and be known by You. In
Jesus' name, amen.

A Solid Foundation

Such is the destiny of all who forget God; so perishes the hope of the godless. What they trust in is fragile; what they rely on is a spider's web. They lean on the web, but it gives way; they cling to it, but it does not hold.

JOB 8:13–15

God, I choose to place my hope in You. I choose to discipline my mind to filter out the messages of discouragement and despair and fear that assault me when the storms of life rage against me. When my circumstances look dark, I will continue walking toward the light. I won't forget You in troubled times, because I have faith in Your almighty sovereignty, Father. And I know that my faith is not misplaced. I can lean on You without fear that You will collapse beneath the load like a fragile spider's web. You are a rock, firm and solid for my foundation. My faith in You gives me hope of new life, a changed heart, and eternity. In the name of Jesus, amen.

Not Forgotten

"Can a mother forget her nursing child? Can she feel no love for the child she has borne? But even if that were possible, I would not forget you! See, I have written your name on the palms of my hands."
Isaiah 49:15–16 NLT

Father, before I knew You, I fell into the trap of feeling unspectacular, unloved, and unnoticed. Those around me were rushing around in their busy lives, and I thought that no one saw my struggles and pains, or even shared in my successes. But then I met You. You love me as a mother loves her newborn child. As soon as that child is born, it's impossible to imagine life without them. You cherish me and think of me often. People will let me down and may overlook me in the crush of their own lives, but You promise never to forget me! You have written my name on the palms of Your hands. Thank You that I am forever in Your thoughts. In Jesus' name, amen.

PURPOSE

We have heard of your faith in Christ Jesus and of the love you have for all God's people—the faith and love that spring from the hope stored up for you in heaven and about which you have already heard in the true message of the gospel.

COLOSSIANS 1:4–5

. . . .

Lord, I know that You have a specific design for my life. You have good plans for me and things You want me to accomplish for You while I'm here on this earth. Help me to wait patiently for Your timing and give me the wisdom to see the path You have marked out for me. It's not always clear to me what tasks I should undertake, but I know that You will make it plain to me in Your time. My hope of salvation and eternity with You in heaven keep me focused on Your purpose. You will never let me go, Father. You know what You are doing, and I don't drift aimlessly through my days when Your purpose propels me. Amen.

THE HOPE OF HEAVEN

And if Christ has not been raised, then your faith is useless and you are still guilty of your sins. In that case, all who have died believing in Christ are lost! And if our hope in Christ is only for this life, we are more to be pitied than anyone in the world.

1 CORINTHIANS 15:17–19 NLT

. . . .

Father God, how pointless and hopeless our lives would be if this world was all there was to look forward to. What hope and joy would we have if the short span of our years here winked out with our final breath and then there was nothing—no glorious streets of gold, no eternity with You and our loved ones in Christ, no greater purpose for our existence than our own selfish ambitions? Without You, we would have no forgiveness or hope of redemption. But You have given us a new hope. The promise of more. The promise of being with You in a perfect place where pain and sin no longer exist. You have given us forever. In Jesus' name, amen.

WE ARE RIGHTEOUS

Abraham never wavered in believing God's promise. In fact, his faith grew stronger, and in this he brought glory to God. He was fully convinced that God is able to do whatever he promises. And because of Abraham's faith, God counted him as righteous. And when God counted him as righteous, it wasn't just for Abraham's benefit. It was recorded for our benefit, too, assuring us that God will also count us as righteous if we believe in him.

ROMANS 4:20–24 NLT

God, Abraham believed Your promises. He believed that You were capable of doing whatever You said You would do. And because he believed You, You saw him as righteous. And You see all believers this way, clean and unblemished in Your eyes. I believe that You sent Jesus here to die on the cross for my sins, that You poured out my punishment on Your spotless Passover Lamb, Your Son. My hope of righteousness lies in my belief that on the third day after His death You, almighty God, raised Him from the dead. And He is alive! He waits for me in heaven, preparing a place for me. And because of His sacrifice, I am counted righteous. In the name of Jesus, amen.

A MIGHTY TREE

Blessed is the one who does not walk in step with the wicked or stand in the way that sinners take or sit in the company of mockers, but whose delight is in the law of the LORD, and who meditates on his law day and night. That person is like a tree planted by streams of water, which yields its fruit in season and whose leaf does not wither—whatever they do prospers.

PSALM 1:1–3

God, the storms of this life rail against me. I want to stand firm, but I don't always. Sometimes I bend and some of my branches break under the pressures and stresses of my trials. But Father, You have promised that if I delight in Your Word and think about it daily and make it part of my life, I will be like a tree by a river, whose roots have grown deep and sprawl wide into the earth. This tree is not easily uprooted and drinks deeply, producing much fruit. Father, may I be unmoved by the howling winds of anxiety, depression, and fear. May I dig deep into Your Word for nourishment and rest in Your strength. In Jesus' name, amen.

GOD OF ALL COMFORT

Praise be to the God and Father of our Lord Jesus Christ, the Father of compassion and the God of all comfort, who comforts us in all our troubles, so that we can comfort those in any trouble with the comfort we ourselves receive from God. For just as we share abundantly in the sufferings of Christ, so also our comfort abounds through Christ.
2 CORINTHIANS 1:3–5

Father, You aren't a distant God who is unmoved by my pain and struggles. You don't remove Yourself from my messy situations. Instead, You step into the middle of my upturned life with compassion and comfort. You soothe my worries and bind up my broken heart. While I might suffer as Jesus did in this world, You minister tenderly to me like the great Shepherd that You are. How wonderful to have a God that I can turn to when I need a hug, when I'm overwhelmed, when I hurt. You shower me in comfort through my hope in Jesus. And now I can take the comfort You have shown me and offer it to those around me. In the name of Jesus, amen.

Worthy of Trust

*May the God of hope fill you with all joy and peace as
you trust in him, so that you may overflow with
hope by the power of the Holy Spirit.*
ROMANS 15:13

. . . .

Lord, You promise great blessings to those who trust in You.
Hebrews 11 is filled with proof that You are trustworthy. Like those
great heroes of faith who have walked before me, I can wholly trust
in Your plans and purposes even when they don't make sense to my
human understanding. Father, I want the joy and peace that accompany trusting You. When You ask me to do something that I don't
understand, may I step forward as a willing vessel in complete trust,
knowing that You have the power to accomplish what You say You
will do and that Your goodness is unparalleled. I praise You, God,
for You have filled me with hope through Jesus. Amen.

REFRESHMENT

*"The LORD is my strength and my defense; he has become
my salvation. He is my God, and I will praise him,
my father's God, and I will exalt him."*

EXODUS 15:2

Father, by the end of each day, I'm ready to collapse. I'm exhausted both physically and spiritually by family life, work, and worry. But how comforting and uplifting to know that I can renew my strength from Your fountain that is ever flowing. Your strength never runs dry. You replenish my soul. In the midst of my daily struggle, it's so easy to be distracted from the promises of Your Word. Sometimes I fail You and fall to temptation. Remind me of Your faithfulness to those who believe. Remind me of Your deep love for me. Remind me that I have hope in Jesus who came to save me, and that this world is not my final home. In Jesus' name, amen.

Hope of Resurrection

"I see that the LORD is always with me. I will not be shaken, for he is right beside me. No wonder my heart is glad, and my tongue shouts his praises! My body rests in hope. For you will not leave my soul among the dead or allow your Holy One to rot in the grave. You have shown me the way of life, and you will fill me with the joy of your presence."
ACTS 2:25–28 NLT

. . . .

Lord, I live in anticipation of the resurrection. You raised Your Son, Jesus, up from the grave, and He lives in heaven now, preparing a place for those who love Him. Imagine the disciples' joy when they saw Jesus alive! They were deep in despair, confusion, and fear at His crucifixion, wondering if they had been wrong about everything. But they had just misunderstood. Your kingdom is not of this world. They must have been flooded with relief and hope and joy to see their Friend and Savior alive again. And You promised to come back for us, Jesus. Death may visit me in this life, but I know that resurrection to new life with You awaits! In the powerful name of Jesus, amen.

A FOREVER HOME

For this world is not our permanent home; we are looking forward to a home yet to come. Therefore, let us offer through Jesus a continual sacrifice of praise to God, proclaiming our allegiance to his name.
HEBREWS 13:14–15 NLT

God, don't allow me to get too comfortable here. When I do, I start enjoying the pleasures and comforts of life a little too much. My eyes wander to the things I can build for myself and the possessions I can accumulate. My efforts stray from building Your kingdom to building my own little empire here in this world. But this place doesn't last. Peter told Your followers to live as strangers in this world, pilgrims who are just passing through. Remind me to keep my bags packed for heaven, that there's a better place I'm waiting for. Right now I'm merely in the prelude to my eternity with You. I live in hopeful anticipation of that forever city. In Jesus' name, amen.

Redeemed

For you know that it was not with perishable things such as silver or gold that you were redeemed from the empty way of life handed down to you from your ancestors, but with the precious blood of Christ, a lamb without blemish or defect. He was chosen before the creation of the world, but was revealed in these last times for your sake.

1 PETER 1:18–20

Lord Jesus, the habits of sin can be so difficult to break. I think I'm maturing in my walk and suddenly I'm blindsided by another misstep. I repeated a cycle of sin I thought I'd left behind. I disappointed You, and I stumbled. I fell hard on my face. But then I look up and see Your nail-pierced hand held out to me. I take it and stand again because You have redeemed me from that empty way of life. For my sake You died, a perfect and unblemished sacrifice to free me from my bonds of sin. Even when I falter, I'm no longer ensnared by my old attitudes and actions, because I'm redeemed. I'm bought by Your blood, and I belong to You. Amen.

WONDERFULLY MADE

I praise you because I am fearfully and wonderfully made; your works are wonderful, I know that full well. My frame was not hidden from you when I was made in the secret place, when I was woven together in the depths of the earth. Your eyes saw my unformed body; all the days ordained for me were written in your book before one of them came to be.
PSALM 139:14–16

Lord, You have made me so amazingly complex. Science is still working to understand the intricacies of the human body and the world You knit together. Not only have You given me a physical body whose workings are astounding, but You've given me a mind that can think and learn and grow and a soul that can love You and live eternally. My mind can't grasp the complexity of Your creation. You saw me when I was being formed in my mother's womb, and You planned out my days before I was ever conceived. You are a God of order and the Master of great planning. You don't leave me to uncertainty and random chance. In Jesus' name, amen.

FOREVER LOVE

"I have loved you, my people, with an everlasting love.
With unfailing love I have drawn you to myself."
JEREMIAH 31:3 NLT

· ·

God, I am loved by You. I have hope through my failures and my struggles because I am assured of Your steadfast love for me. In this world, love can be a confusing concept. Parents might say they love us but have time only for themselves. Their selfish love warps our understanding of what love is. A spouse or friend might tell us they love us but then walk away if we mess up too badly. Their conditional love leaves us shaky. But You, Father, promise that Your love is everlasting and unfailing. Your love isn't selfish or conditional. I can't earn my way into Your affection. You loved me always, even before I was born. Others may walk away from me, but Your love stands forever. Amen.

Draw Near

He gives us more grace. That is why Scripture says: "God opposes the proud but shows favor to the humble." Submit yourselves, then, to God. Resist the devil, and he will flee from you. Come near to God and he will come near to you.

JAMES 4:6–8

. . . .

Father, *submit* and *humble* are two words I cringe at reading in Your Word. Just like running into a coffee table in the dark, I've cracked the battered shins of my soul against the hard edge of my pride on numerous occasions. But You give grace generously to the humble. I have hope that through the power of Your Holy Spirit who dwells in me I can learn to quell my pride. I submit myself to You, Lord. I will resist Satan's attempts to convince me that my wants and needs are more important than others'. Purify my heart. Show me the hidden stains of pride. Thank You, Father, that I can come closer to You and know that You will be there. Amen.

HE'S COMING BACK

For the Lord himself will come down from heaven, with a loud command, with the voice of the archangel and with the trumpet call of God, and the dead in Christ will rise first. After that, we who are still alive and are left will be caught up together with them in the clouds to meet the Lord in the air. And so we will be with the Lord forever. Therefore encourage one another with these words.

1 THESSALONIANS 4:16–18

. . . .

Lord Jesus, the thought of Your return makes hope rise within me. You will call all the believers to You in the clouds. The trials and anxieties of this world will fall away as I rise to meet with You, my Friend, my Savior. At times I question whether my struggles are worth it, but when I see You, Jesus, I will know that every tear, every hardship, every internal struggle with my sinful nature will have been so worth it. Forever with You is worth the battle. I will continue to fight the good fight so I can win the race and gain my crown. Jesus, I can't wait to meet You in the clouds. Amen.

Forgiven

If we claim to be without sin, we deceive ourselves and the truth is not in us. If we confess our sins, he is faithful and just and will forgive us our sins and purify us from all unrighteousness. If we claim we have not sinned, we make him out to be a liar and his word is not in us.

1 John 1:8–10

Lord, You are faithful to forgive us when we confess to You. Oh, how sweet the balm of forgiveness soothes my battered soul when I know that I've messed up. I know I am a sinner with no hope of being perfect in this life. I do selfish things. I hurt other people. I walk away from You sometimes, God. But when I come to You and say I'm sorry, You will always forgive me. I am unworthy of such acceptance, but You shower me in grace and mercy nonetheless. Help me to extend Your brand of forgiveness to others. I release any anger or grudges I've been holding, because You have forgiven me all my sins. In Jesus' name, amen.

HE HEARS ME

The LORD hears his people when they call to him for help. He rescues them from all their troubles. The LORD is close to the brokenhearted; he rescues those whose spirits are crushed. The righteous person faces many troubles, but the LORD comes to the rescue each time.
PSALM 34:17–19 NLT

Father, You are the God who hears me. I'm so grateful that I never have to wonder if You are listening when I bring my problems to You. When I'm feeling down I can talk to You about it. I can open Your Word and You speak to me with encouragement. When my heart is broken, You are near, Father. You soothe me with words of comfort. Others may not have time to listen when I need to pour out my heart and sort through my emotions, but You always have time for this daughter of Yours. You are always full of wisdom and help me decide which way to turn, whether to take action or to be still and allow You to work. Amen.

He Satisfies

You, God, are my God, earnestly I seek you; I thirst for you, my whole being longs for you, in a dry and parched land where there is no water. I have seen you in the sanctuary and beheld your power and your glory. Because your love is better than life, my lips will glorify you. I will praise you as long as I live.

PSALM 63:1–4

. . . .

Lord, this world can feel like a barren desert, offering nothing that will satisfy the longings of my soul. I have tried to fill myself up with its comforts and pleasures, but ultimately they leave me feeling empty and alone. Success is cold comfort when I'm struggling or hurting. Money is fleeting and lasts only for this lifetime. I was longing for something more. But then I found You, my God. You held out a cup of living water that saturated my desiccated soul with new life—everlasting life. And You love me. I have found the "more" that I was seeking. It's You. You have repaired my broken places and forgiven my sins. I can't stop praising You for how You have saved me. Amen.

I Am Clean

Let us go right into the presence of God with sincere hearts fully trusting him. For our guilty consciences have been sprinkled with Christ's blood to make us clean, and our bodies have been washed with pure water. Let us hold tightly without wavering to the hope we affirm, for God can be trusted to keep his promise. Let us think of ways to motivate one another to acts of love and good works.
HEBREWS 10:22–24 NLT

Father, I am clean! I can walk right into Your throne room and know You because Jesus has scrubbed away all the dirt and grime of my failures and misdeeds. I have grabbed ahold of Your promises and the hope You've given me, and I am not letting go. The enemy may try to convince me that You aren't going to keep Your promises, but I know that You are trustworthy. Through the generations, not a single promise of Yours has been broken. My faith will persevere through the trials I endure because I trust the lifeline I'm clinging to. Father, use me to provoke others to work hard to spread the awesome news of Your love. In Jesus' precious name, amen.

The Good Stuff

I will be fully satisfied as with the richest of foods;
with singing lips my mouth will praise you.
PSALM 63:5

. . . .

Lord, I have been hungry for something different and more than the things I've been living for. I've allowed idols to gain my affections. I've sacrificed time with You and our relationship so that I could hold on to other things that ultimately haven't satisfied me. I no longer want to forfeit the fullness of Your grace because I'm clinging to my idols. Forgive me for my unfaithfulness. I'm longing for the good stuff. I've found that with You, Lord. My favorite meal gives me both pleasure and satisfaction. Praise You, Lord, I have tasted Your delectable nature and have seen that You are good. May I never use false substitutes for You in my life again. In the name of Jesus, amen.

He Speaks Tenderly

"She decked herself with rings and jewelry, and went after her lovers, but me she forgot," declares the LORD. "Therefore I am now going to allure her; I will lead her into the wilderness and speak tenderly to her. There I will give her back her vineyards, and will make the Valley of Achor a door of hope. There she will respond as in the days of her youth."

HOSEA 2:13–15

Father, I have chased after other loves in my life. I have cheated on Your great love for me with selfishness and deliberate disobedience. I have squandered time on myself and ignored Your requests. And yet, instead of berating me for my wrong choices and condemning me for my mistakes, You choose to woo me back to You with tender words. You take me into the desert so I can be alone with You. You are jealous of my affections and want my full attention. The desert may seem barren and lonely, but You are always near. You don't abandon me there, but rather, You want me to praise You even in the wilderness. You are moving in my life even when I can't see You. Amen.

GAIN LIFE

"Whoever wants to be my disciple must deny themselves and take up their cross daily and follow me. For whoever wants to save their life will lose it, but whoever loses their life for me will save it. What good is it for someone to gain the whole world, and yet lose or forfeit their very self?"

LUKE 9:23–25

. . . .

Lord, the cross led You into death, and You would have me follow You there—the death of my self, of my sin. Following You is a daily choice of surrender to follow Your lead and not go my own way. The world doesn't understand why I would give up myself to serve You, Jesus. They don't know what You did for me. Surrender can be excruciating, just as Calvary was for You. Dying is never easy. And dying to my own pride and selfishness is no different. But You promise me something so much greater. By enslaving myself to righteousness, my life is saved. I have given it to You, and You have given me back eternity and real living today. In Jesus' name, amen.

A New Way of Thinking

*Finally, brothers and sisters, whatever is true, whatever is noble,
whatever is right, whatever is pure, whatever is lovely, whatever is
admirable—if anything is excellent or praiseworthy—think about
such things. Whatever you have learned or received or
heard from me, or seen in me—put it into practice.
And the God of peace will be with you.*
PHILIPPIANS 4:8–9

Lord, I've been stuck in critical and judgmental thinking. Negative thoughts about myself and others swirl in my head. It makes me grumpy and unhappy when I allow unimportant stuff to bother me. But You have given me a solution, a new way of thinking. I choose to dwell on the positive. I will scour my surroundings for the true and lovely. I will focus on my husband's positive attributes instead of his flaws. I will praise my children when they're kind and loving instead of constantly chastising their mistakes. I will find the blessings stirred in with my unpleasant circumstances. Thank You, Jesus, for renewing my mind. Help me to practice what I have learned from You. In Jesus' name, amen.

Take Out the Trash

But whatever were gains to me I now consider loss for the sake of Christ. What is more, I consider everything a loss because of the surpassing worth of knowing Christ Jesus my Lord, for whose sake I have lost all things. I consider them garbage, that I may gain Christ and be found in him, not having a righteousness of my own that comes from the law, but that which is through faith in Christ.
PHILIPPIANS 3:7–9

Father, what worldly things do I value? Show me the areas in my life where I have elevated worthless things above their station. Money, acceptance, social status, pride, my home, my job—none of these things can save me or make me acceptable in Your eyes. The apostle Paul discovered that even rigorously following the Law could not bring him righteousness. Help me put my garbage in its place. I want You, Jesus, and only You. Nothing else matters except knowing that I belong to You. My hope and righteousness arise from my faith in You. May I measure everything I allow into my life against the standard of knowing You and rid my life of worthless garbage and distractions. In the name of Jesus, amen.

A NEW KIND OF FRUIT

*But the fruit of the Spirit is love, joy, peace, forbearance, kindness,
goodness, faithfulness, gentleness and self-control. Against such things
there is no law. Those who belong to Christ Jesus have crucified the
flesh with its passions and desires. Since we live by the Spirit,
let us keep in step with the Spirit. Let us not become
conceited, provoking and envying each other.*
GALATIANS 5:22–26

Jesus, since I met You, I'm living a new life—a life led by the
Holy Spirit. Instead of indulging whatever sinful urge enters my
mind, I'm following the direction of Your Spirit. And I'm seeing
the good results, the delicious evidence of the Spirit's work in
my life. Instead of the rottenness of anxiety and unhappiness, I
have tasted the sweetness of joy and peace and love. When I am
tempted toward anger, Your Spirit nudges me to patience. When
I want to lash out in spite when I'm slighted, I remember Your
kindness. Before, I thought the status quo was the only way, now I
know that I can nail my sinful nature to Your cross and walk away.
I can walk in step with Your Spirit. Amen.

Rely on His Love

This is how we know that we live in him and he in us: He has given us of his Spirit. And we have seen and testify that the Father has sent his Son to be the Savior of the world. If anyone acknowledges that Jesus is the Son of God, God lives in them and they in God. And so we know and rely on the love God has for us.

1 John 4:13–16

Lord, it's so amazing that I can know Your love. I can lean on it when I'm feeling weak and know that it will not give way beneath me. Your love for me is reliable. You're not going to take it back if I mess up. How incredible that when I acknowledge Jesus as my Savior and Your Son, You live in me, God, by sending me Your Spirit. The holy and perfect, all-powerful God lives in me. The apostle John wrote that he saw with his own eyes that You sent Jesus to die for our sins. I never have to doubt the truth of Your Gospel or the veracity of Your love. I put my trust in Your love. In Jesus' name, amen.

MORE THAN CONQUERORS

No, in all these things we are more than conquerors through him who loved us. For I am convinced that neither death nor life, neither angels nor demons, neither the present nor the future, nor any powers, neither height nor depth, nor anything else in all creation, will be able to separate us from the love of God that is in Christ Jesus our Lord.

ROMANS 8:37–39

Father, Romans 8:34–35 explains "all these things" that we've conquered through Jesus. It talks about hardship and trouble and persecution, famine and nakedness and danger. We've conquered them because You love us. Nothing in all creation can rip Your love from me. And because of that, I can be victorious in hope whether I am suffering from a loss or an illness, whether I am in fear of danger, or if I am in need. No one can condemn me, because Jesus is my forgiver and my interceder with You. You didn't spare Jesus, Your own Son, so why would I doubt that You will graciously give me all that I need? With You I'm not just barely surviving, I'm conquering. In the name of Jesus, amen.

He Is Patient

But do not forget this one thing, dear friends: With the Lord a day is like a thousand years, and a thousand years are like a day. The Lord is not slow in keeping his promise, as some understand slowness. Instead he is patient with you, not wanting anyone to perish, but everyone to come to repentance.

2 Peter 3:8–9

God, Your amazing capacity for patience gives me great hope. Waiting is never easy. I always want to speed things up and have everything now, now, now. But You have the ability to wait for Your plans to work. You wait for the seeds sown in my life to take root and grow into maturity. You don't expect overnight growth. Instead, You keep watering those seeds and feeding them until one day they sprout. You gently and patiently teach me with kindness. You love us enough to wait for us to come to You in repentance. You don't want to lose any of us. The answer to why You don't just return right now and stop this messed-up world is love and patience. In Jesus' name, amen.

KNOW THE WAY

"You know the way to the place where I am going." Thomas said to him, "Lord, we don't know where you are going, so how can we know the way?" Jesus answered, "I am the way and the truth and the life. No one comes to the Father except through me. If you really know me, you will know my Father as well. From now on, you do know him and have seen him."

JOHN 14:4–7

Father, our world is filled with mixed signals and fake "truths." I've been lost and confused before. I probably will be again. But because I have chosen to follow Jesus, I now know the way to the place where I am going. I can make the right decisions and separate truth from lies. I don't have to flounder in confusion over the meaning of life—because the answer is to know You! I have met the Way and the Truth and the Life in person, and through Him I have come to know You better and have seen Your face. Thank You, Jesus, for becoming the way that we could gain access to God and see Him. In the precious name of Jesus, amen.

HANGING ON THE VINE

"I am the true vine, and my Father is the gardener. He cuts off every branch in me that bears no fruit, while every branch that does bear fruit he prunes so that it will be even more fruitful. You are already clean because of the word I have spoken to you. Remain in me, as I also remain in you. No branch can bear fruit by itself; it must remain in the vine."
JOHN 15:1–4

Lord, pruning my bushes is messy business. Cast-off, withered branches and dead leaves will litter the ground when You're finished. But ultimately, when my landscape comes into full bloom this spring, it will be beautiful and healthy because of the trimming work You've done. Cutting off the dead allows the healthy branches to flourish. Father, You are my vine dresser. Snip off all of my dead habits, every sinful compulsion, that doesn't bear fruit in my life for You. I know that without all the dead weight of old habits and selfish desires, I will mature in my faith and bear the succulent fruit of Your Spirit. To abide in You I must stay in Your presence always—through prayer, Your Word, and my Christian family. Amen.

He's Big Enough

Humble yourselves, therefore, under God's mighty hand, that he may lift you up in due time. Cast all your anxiety on him because he cares for you. Be alert and of sober mind. Your enemy the devil prowls around like a roaring lion looking for someone to devour. Resist him, standing firm in the faith.

1 Peter 5:6–9

Father God, I need a strong shoulder, something sturdy and unmovable to lean on. Without You in my life, I'm consumed with worry, anxiety, and fears. Without You, I'm left with nothing but my own inadequate attempts to cope with my hurts and my uncertainty. Without You, I have no assurance of something greater. But You are here. And You are big enough to handle all of my emotions. I can throw my fears onto Your capable shoulders. Because You care. My consolation stems from the knowledge that You care. A mighty yet unfeeling God would be cold comfort to my anxiety. But I am at peace because You tenderly attend to every detail of Your plan. In the name of Jesus, amen.

Not Conquered

Then, accompanied by the disciples, Jesus left the upstairs room and went as usual to the Mount of Olives. There he told them, "Pray that you will not give in to temptation."
LUKE 22:39–40 NLT

God, Jesus knew the awful struggle we would endure with temptation. His time in the desert taught Him how we would wrestle with our inner desires and the compulsion to be driven by our fears. The night before His crucifixion, He gently warned His disciples to pray that they would persevere because He knew of the terrifying night and days ahead of them. Mother Teresa wrote, "Don't be surprised at your failure. We must connect every bit of our life with Holy Communion; all our failures, our weakness, our pride and our misery. See that, in spite of being tempted, you are not conquered."[3] I praise You, Jesus, that even though I've failed as spectacularly as Peter did that night, like him, I am not conquered. Amen.

3 Mother Teresa, *Where There Is Love, There Is God*, ed. Brian Kolodiejchuk (New York: Image, 2010), 113.

MAGNIFICENT PERFECTION

The heavens proclaim the glory of God. The skies display his
craftsmanship. Day after day they continue to speak; night after
night they make him known. They speak without a sound or
word; their voice is never heard. Yet their message has gone
throughout the earth, and their words to all the world. . . .
The instructions of the LORD are perfect, reviving the soul.
PSALM 19:1–4, 7 NLT

God of the universe, You are perfection. This world screams Your magnificence and glory at the top of its lungs with the first blush of every morning. All I have to do is listen to the voice of Your creation. The dictionary says that to be perfect is to be flawless and complete, thoroughly skilled or proficient, pure and undiluted. And because perfection is encompassed in Your character, Your guidelines are also perfect. I trust in the utter flawlessness of Your plans and the purity of Your laws. For they can be nothing less, since to be lacking anything would contradict Your perfection. My hope is bolstered by the knowledge that I serve a God incapable of making a mistake. In Jesus' name, amen.

He Draws Near

We had no rest, but we were harassed at every turn—conflicts on the outside, fears within. But God, who comforts the downcast, comforted us by the coming of Titus, and not only by his coming but also by the comfort you had given him. He told us about your longing for me, your deep sorrow, your ardent concern for me, so that my joy was greater than ever.

2 Corinthians 7:5–7

. . . .

Lord, I can relate to Paul's feelings in this passage. I have suffered external conflicts, whether with people or circumstances, and been assaulted internally by my fears. My mind has raged in battle with my anxiety, and I've felt far from You. I've been harassed and condemned because I follow You. But I know that the word Paul used here for comfort means "to draw near or come alongside." When I need Your help, You come close to me, just as You have drawn near to others in their times of trial throughout the ages. It is a great comfort to know that You will be here beside me when I need You and lend me the strength I need to get through the hard times. Amen.

A POWERFUL SPIRIT

For this reason I remind you to fan into flame the gift of God, which is in you through the laying on of my hands. For the Spirit God gave us does not make us timid, but gives us power, love and self-discipline.
2 TIMOTHY 1:6–7

Lord, remind me when I feel powerless that Your Spirit is anything but weak. I've boxed You up neatly before, underestimated You, and corralled You to certain acceptable areas of my life. I've devoted some quiet time to You when I have a spare moment and have gone to church, but You are so much more than a Sunday God. You've given me the gift of Your Spirit. Because You live in me, I can walk out a bold and brave faith. The enemy would prefer that I stay ineffectual by keeping You inside a box, but You have called me to live a faith of power, love, and self-discipline. Your Spirit, with all the mighty power of the living, eternal God, lives in me. Amen.

Forever the Same

*Remember your leaders, who spoke the word of God to you. Consider
the outcome of their way of life and imitate their faith. Jesus Christ
is the same yesterday and today and forever. Do not be carried away
by all kinds of strange teachings. It is good for our hearts to
be strengthened by grace, not by eating ceremonial foods,
which is of no benefit to those who do so.*

HEBREWS 13:7–9

Father, the fads of this world change faster than I can adapt—
clothing trends shift from wide-legged pants to skinny jeans;
numerous diets come and go, Atkins to South Beach to Whole 30,
who can keep up? But in a world that's swirling in change, there is a
constant as old as eternity. You, Lord, do not shift. You're comfort-
ingly always the same as You were yesterday. And You'll still be the
same tomorrow as You are today. Your Word does not alter. I can
hold any "trendy" new belief against the ageless pillar of scripture
and determine its truth. Your unshifting character brings hope to
my faith, because Your promises of old will forever be upheld. In
Jesus' name, amen.

Known and Loved

You have searched me, LORD, and you know me. You know when I sit and when I rise; you perceive my thoughts from afar. You discern my going out and my lying down; you are familiar with all my ways. Before a word is on my tongue you, LORD, know it completely. You hem me in behind and before, and you lay your hand upon me.

PSALM 139:1–5

God, great libraries would overflow with the things about You that I *don't* know. In my meager human years, I could never aspire to fully know You. But You know me. You know everything there is to know about me, from my deepest thought to every freckle on my skin. You know my character and my actions. You're familiar with each and every habit I entertain. You know how I like my coffee, and You also plumb the depths of my love for You. You see the good in me, and my darkest moments are revealed to You. And yet, knowing all the secrets about me that You do, You still rest Your guiding hand of love upon me. Thank You, Jesus, amen.

Adorn the Humble

Let them praise his name with dancing and make music to him
with timbrel and harp. For the LORD takes delight in his people;
he crowns the humble with victory. Let his faithful people
rejoice in this honor and sing for joy on their beds.

PSALM 149:3–5

Father, I used to think I was a pretty good person. If the church doors were open, I was there. I helped people and volunteered my time. I'm sure my friends and family would have said I was honest and trustworthy, kind and generous. I thought I had nothing to worry about because I did all the right things. My pride clouded my view of myself—until I read, "For all have sinned and fall short of the glory of God," and "the gift of God is eternal life" (Romans 3:23; 6:23). For the first time, I heard about Your grace. Not my effort, but Your gift. You crown the humble with salvation. Not the haughty who think they're superior, but those of us willing to admit our unworthiness. Amen.

Up from the Depths

Your righteousness, God, reaches to the heavens, you who have done great things. Who is like you, God? Though you have made me see troubles, many and bitter, you will restore my life again; from the depths of the earth you will again bring me up.

Psalm 71:19–20

Lord, our problems can lead us down a rutted road of discouragement and bitterness. We can get caught up in wanting to escape our unpleasant circumstances instead of looking for You there. We seldom want to remain long enough to be refined by our trials. But I have hope in Your righteousness, God. You long for me to become more like Jesus more than You want me to live a comfortable life. And when I've been changed and shaped for the better, You're waiting to restore me. My hard places are not devoid of hope, merely tools in Your hand—a barren desert stripped of distraction where I can meet You. You have done spectacular things, and You will do amazing work in me too. In Jesus' name, amen.

ABUNDANT PEACE

Soon the wicked will disappear. Though you look for them, they will be gone. The lowly will possess the land and will live in peace and prosperity.

PSALM 37:10–11 NLT

. . . .

Heavenly Father, wars, strife, fear, torn-up families, lying politicians—our world could be described in one word: *broken*. We've all suffered. But You haven't left us in shards with no hope. Instead, You sent Jesus to save us and teach us how to live the Kingdom lifestyle. Entering into Your grace requires us to pass through the doors of meekness. But You promise those who humble themselves before You an inheritance where wickedness and evil no longer exist, a place where we can thrive in abundant peace, where not another teardrop will fall. No more relationships will shatter, and death will abdicate its throne. A place where fear is but a distant, forgotten emotion. A place where You are. In the name of Jesus, amen.

Unimaginably More

Now to him who is able to do immeasurably more than all we ask or imagine, according to his power that is at work within us, to him be glory in the church and in Christ Jesus throughout all generations, for ever and ever! Amen.

EPHESIANS 3:20–21

Lord, praying to You is easier than calling a friend for a chat. In the midst of this accessibility, sometimes I forget how amazing that is—I can pray to the living God. You will listen to me! And You're not just a sympathetic ear. Your Word says that You have the power to do immeasurably more than all I ask or imagine. Help me to pray expectantly and passionately and continually to the only One who can really change things. Your fantastic power is working within me. Keep working on me until I become the daughter You desire. And when my answers don't seem to be exactly what I'd hoped for, help me remember that You imagine more and think bigger than I do. Amen.

CLEAR THE WAY

Night and day we pray most earnestly that we may see you again and supply what is lacking in your faith. Now may our God and Father himself and our Lord Jesus clear the way for us to come to you.

1 THESSALONIANS 3:10–11

God, I don't see a way forward through all the problems assaulting me. Everything I attempt ends in utter failure. How am I to move forward? Show me the way, because You are the great Way Maker. You can bust down the walls in my path. You can remove the obstacles that hinder my journey. When all seems hopeless, You alone can clear the way. You have the power to open avenues I never imagined possible. Supply what is lacking in my faith and trust. I'm waiting expectantly for You to make a game-changing move. I will ask continually until I see the path You have prepared for me. In the powerful name of Jesus, amen.

RADIANT

I sought the LORD, and he answered me; he delivered me
from all my fears. Those who look to him are radiant;
their faces are never covered with shame.

PSALM 34:4–5

. . . .

Father, I have felt shame. I have done things that I don't want anyone to see. I wish I could hide them and never think of them again. Their stain taints my life. I kick my thoughts of them to the dark corners, but You already know all about everything I've ever done, every misstep, every sin, every regret. And yet You still want me! You've forgiven me. You answered when I went looking for You, and You've delivered me from shame and replaced my sorrow with radiance. Instead of outcast and rejection, You've given me a new name. You've called me precious daughter, the apple of Your eye. I no longer feel ashamed. I'm glowing with Your love and approval. In Jesus' name, amen.

SCENT OF LIFE

But thanks be to God, who always leads us as captives in Christ's
triumphal procession and uses us to spread the aroma of the knowledge
of him everywhere. For we are to God the pleasing aroma of Christ
among those who are being saved and those who are perishing.
To the one we are an aroma that brings death;
to the other, an aroma that brings life.
2 CORINTHIANS 2:14–16

Heavenly Father, spring smells so good. I step outside into the welcoming sunshine and I'm compelled to inhale deeply the fragrance of new life. Flowers and fresh-cut grass perfume the breeze. It gives me hope of warm and pleasant summer days to come after the harsh deadness of winter. Like a fresh spring morning, Your followers are a pleasing aroma to You. Like a walking bouquet of fragrant blooms, we spread the aroma of the knowledge of You all around. You smile and breathe in the scent of new life in You. Make my words and actions a pleasing incense to You today. May they lead others into the everlasting life of knowing You. In the name of Jesus, amen.

Superior Weapons

We are human, but we don't wage war as humans do. We use God's mighty weapons, not worldly weapons, to knock down the strongholds of human reasoning and to destroy false arguments. We destroy every proud obstacle that keeps people from knowing God. We capture their rebellious thoughts and teach them to obey Christ.

2 Corinthians 10:3–5 NLT

God, You haven't left us defenseless in this world. Far from it, You've outfitted us with divine weapons because we're fighting a war for our eternal souls. Our enemy wants to keep us from knowing You. He would deceive us into believing lies about You. But You have given us faith as our shield against hopelessness, truth as our belt, salvation as our helmet, righteousness as our body armor, and Your Spirit and Your Word to engage the enemy in combat. You taught us how to capture our rebellious thoughts and make them obedient to You. Thank You for Your protection and provision for the spiritual battle we endure. Keep my mind locked on You so I may gain victory today. In Jesus' name, amen.

Strength Out of Weakness

"My grace is all you need. My power works best in weakness."
So now I am glad to boast about my weaknesses, so that the power
of Christ can work through me. That's why I take pleasure in my
weaknesses, and in the insults, hardships, persecutions, and troubles
that I suffer for Christ. For when I am weak, then I am strong.

2 Corinthians 12:9–10 NLT

Lord, I don't have to be strong for You. And I don't need to have it all together to be used by You. In fact, my pride is a stumbling block to Your power. You value those who admit their short-comings, those who are humble enough to recognize their need for You. When I am weak, I am strong with the power of Christ. Otherwise I might be tempted to take credit for things You've done. I shouldn't complain about my weaknesses or see them as punishments from an angry God. Instead, they're gifts to help me experience more of Your power. Help me to rejoice in my weakness as Paul did so I may live powerfully through You. In the name of Jesus, amen.

CHOSEN TO LOVE

A servant does not know his master's business. Instead, I have called you friends, for everything that I learned from my Father I have made known to you. You did not choose me, but I chose you and appointed you so that you might go and bear fruit—fruit that will last—and so that whatever you ask in my name the Father will give you. This is my command: Love each other.

JOHN 15:15–17

. . . .

Father, too often I haven't chosen You with my actions. Instead I've betrayed You, as Judas did. I've sold You out for the glittering silver of my own desires, my comfort, my glory, and my own self-seeking gain. But that isn't the end of the story. Yes, Judas betrayed You with a kiss, but You still chose him, even when You knew his love for You wouldn't be true. And You've chosen me as well, not because I chose You, but because You love me. You appointed me to bear lasting fruit. You called me friend instead of enemy. Lord, help me to choose You back—to choose to love others instead of self. In Jesus' name, amen.

GOD'S GRACE

The Lamb who was slain from the creation of the world.
REVELATION 13:8

. . . .

Father God, Your grace is too much. It's free and undeserved and unlimited. I wonder that You can offer it to wretches like us, and yet You do! Every time I need it, which is mostly every second of every day, I never reach its end because everything about You is infinite. A. W. Tozer wrote, "Grace is God's goodness, the kindness of God's heart, the good will, the cordial benevolence. It is what God is like. God is like that all the time. You'll never run into a stratum in God that is hard. You'll always find God gracious, at all times and toward all peoples forever."[4] Thank You for Your plan of grace from the foundation of the world. In Jesus' name, amen.

4 A.W. Tozer, *The Attributes of God* (Chicago: Wingspread Publishers, 2003), 103.

A New Family

For you are all children of God through faith in Christ Jesus. And all who have been united with Christ in baptism have put on Christ, like putting on new clothes. There is no longer Jew or Gentile, slave or free, male and female. For you are all one in Christ Jesus. And now that you belong to Christ, you are the true children of Abraham. You are his heirs, and God's promise to Abraham belongs to you.

GALATIANS 3:26–29 NLT

. . . .

God, some of us hail from families with impressive legacies, and some of us have no family to speak of—or none we want to speak of anyway. And while I can't choose my earthly family, I can choose Yours! I can become Your true child, with the legacy of promises and inheritance that awaits everyone in Your family. And even better, it's not just an eternal inheritance I wait for, but a brand-new family here on earth. I gain brothers and sisters galore. There are no class or race or gender divisions in Your family—we're all one in You. Help me to promote unity in my church family and be an uplifting support to my siblings in Christ. In Jesus' name, amen.

CLEANSED

*Don't you realize that this is not the way to live? Unjust people who
don't care about God will not be joining in his kingdom. Those who
use and abuse each other, use and abuse sex, use and abuse the earth
and everything in it, don't qualify as citizens in God's kingdom.
A number of you know from experience what I'm talking about,
for not so long ago you were on that list. Since then, you've been
cleaned up and given a fresh start by Jesus, our Master,
our Messiah, and by our God present in us, the Spirit.*
1 CORINTHIANS 6:9–11 MSG

Father in heaven, I feel the filth of my sin. I am well acquainted with
the shame that comes with being considered dirty and unworthy.
I've knowingly done things that are wrong in Your eyes. But You
have plunged me into a clear spring of water. Your Son's blood has
scoured away all of my sin until I'm sparkling and pristine before
You. I no longer need to hide my ratty rags in the darkness. Instead,
I step into the light and come closer to You, assured by my faith
in You that I have been washed and purified. You no longer see
my past. Instead, You see me draped in robes of holiness. My con-
science is clean! In Jesus' name, amen.

COURSE CORRECTION

Search me, God, and know my heart; test me and know my
anxious thoughts. See if there is any offensive way
in me, and lead me in the way everlasting.
PSALM 139:23–24

. . . .

God, without using their instruments to correct their flight path, pilots would never safely arrive at their destination and most likely would end up in a blazing fireball on the ground. I too need direction and guidance. Sometimes I get confused by the messages peddled by this world. On my own, I'm flying blind during the dark nights and foggy conditions I encounter. But You can lead me through. Thank You for Your Word and Your Holy Spirit who teaches and corrects me. Help me not to rebel against Your discipline, because without it, I too would end up in a flaming crash of failure. Instead, help me to see the deep and abiding love that drives Your discipline. In the name of Jesus, amen.

His Story of Hope

*For everything that was written in the past was written to teach us,
so that through the endurance taught in the Scriptures and
the encouragement they provide we might have hope.*

ROMANS 15:4

God, just when it looks like the good guys are poised on the brink of failure, my favorite super-hero charges onto the screen. Who doesn't love a good fantasy? They encourage us to strive for more in our own lives—more courage, more honor, more strength. It's fun to imagine new worlds, even though, in the end, they're not real. But the Bible is not just another collection of fairy tales. Every word of scripture is true and effective for teaching and encouragement. Thank You for writing down Your great story of the ages! You knew without it, we would slip into despair. So You penned Your love and Your plans for us to spur us by hope toward endurance. In Jesus' name, amen.

COMFORTED

"As a mother comforts her child, so will I comfort you; and you will be comforted over Jerusalem." When you see this, your heart will rejoice and you will flourish like grass; the hand of the LORD will be made known to his servants.

ISAIAH 66:13–14

Father, when a child cries out in the night a mother's instinct is to shush and cuddle her closely, to sing a lullaby, to assure—to comfort. She wants to ease her angst or pain and calm her fears, to restore rightness to her child's world and bring peace to her little mind and rest to her tired body. At times, I need all of these assurances too. I know that when I walk through the dark valleys, Your presence will comfort me. I am sheltered under the shadow of Your mighty wings, held close to Your side. Your peace that passes all understanding soothes my mind and heart. Your deep and tender love envelops me like a warm blanket. In Jesus' name, amen.

Dwelling with Glory

The Word became flesh and made his dwelling among us. We have seen his glory, the glory of the one and only Son, who came from the Father, full of grace and truth. (John testified concerning him. He cried out, saying, "This is the one I spoke about when I said, 'He who comes after me has surpassed me because he was before me.' ")

John 1:14–15

. . . .

Lord, You didn't have to lower Yourself to our position. You didn't have to take on our humble and limited human form as a helpless baby and live among us—but You did. Just as Adam and Eve experienced in the garden, You brought us once again face-to-face with the glory of God. You dwelt among us, lived in our shabby homes, and worked calluses into Your hands. You loved us enough to come where we were when we couldn't reach You and deliver us into Your grace and truth. I'm amazed at Your willingness to step down, to set aside Your high position and serve one such as I. And not just to serve, but to take my place in death. All for love. All for me. Amen.

CHOSEN

*For he chose us in him before the creation of the world to be holy
and blameless in his sight. In love he predestined us for adoption
to sonship through Jesus Christ, in accordance with his
pleasure and will—to the praise of his glorious grace,
which he has freely given us in the One he loves.*

 EPHESIANS 1:4–6

Father, I've been snubbed. I've been abandoned. I've been left out by friends and rejected by family. I've felt insignificant and unimportant, overlooked and neglected. My self-worth plummeted with each new slight. But Your Word tells me that I'm more than a castaway creation. Your Word says that I *have* been chosen—by You. I may have been orphaned by this world, but You picked me to be Your precious daughter and adopted me into Your family. There I have found acceptance and grace unlimited. I have found a place to belong and be loved for all eternity. I've discovered a Father who loves me and sees me as holy and blameless and cherished, even when no one else wanted me. In Jesus' name, amen.

MY ROCK

"There is no one holy like the LORD;
there is no one besides you; there is no Rock like our God."
1 SAMUEL 2:2

. . . .

Lord, life is so uncertain. We're not guaranteed anything more than the fleeting moment we're living right now. Fortunes have been lost in a blink and tragedy can strike anywhere, anytime. When I take my focus off of You, my precarious position leaves me on edge, waiting for the next bad thing to hit. But I don't need to wring my hands in worry. I have You—the singular and mighty God. You are the bedrock of my soul. My high ground during the raging storms. My unshakable foundation when the world trembles. There is no rock like You. As long as I follow You, I have Your assurance that no matter what curve-ball life pitches at me, my feet will be planted firmly on stable ground. Amen.

No Gimmicks

"Peace I leave with you; my peace I give you. I do not give to you as the world gives. Do not let your hearts be troubled and do not be afraid."

JOHN 14:27

. . . .

Lord, if something looks too good to be true, we know that it usually is. Why? Because in this fallen world, it seems that everyone, no matter how altruistic their actions appear, has ulterior motives or a self-serving angle. Is anyone truly selfless and good? Only You. The hidden strings of this world are absent from Your gifts. You give out of pure, unadulterated love. Your gifts are real, not an illusion. Your peace is legitimate and substantial. It won't break down two hours after the warranty expires. It's truly unlimited coverage, and it permeates every facet of my life, coating me in the calm of Your love. Lord, make me a genuine article in Your likeness. Let me give freely, expecting nothing. In Jesus' name, amen.

No Excuse

For ever since the world was created, people have seen the earth and sky. Through everything God made, they can clearly see his invisible qualities—his eternal power and divine nature. So they have no excuse for not knowing God.

ROMANS 1:20 NLT

Father, You gave us the evidence we crave. It stretches before our eyes each morning when the sun's rays unfurl across the horizon. It's there in the fire of a fall forest. It's there in the complexity of each unique flake of snow fluttering down. It's there in the tender spring blooms that slowly raise their faces toward heaven. It's there in the deep sapphire of a summer sky. You painted the world with the proof of Your invisible qualities. Only a divine God of eternal power could accomplish what You've done. You exist. You're here. And You love us. You've left us no excuse for not knowing You—we just have to open our eyes and see! In the name of Jesus, amen.

God's Longing

Yet the LORD longs to be gracious to you; therefore he will rise up to show you compassion. For the LORD is a God of justice. Blessed are all who wait for him!

ISAIAH 30:18

. . . .

God, I don't need creamy chocolate ice cream sprinkled with delicious bits of chewy chocolate truffle—and maybe drizzled with fudge. It's not essential to my nutrition, and I'm certainly not starving. But did I mention it was chocolate? I just really, really want it. It's amazing to me that You, the God of everything, want to be with me and long to be gracious to me. Even when I betray You, Your love for me remains faithful and true. The depth of Your compassion is unfathomable to me. I'm unworthy of Your grace, and yet Your desire for me to have it surpasses even my mammoth chocolate cravings. Prepare my heart with repentance so I can walk in Your grace. In the name of Jesus, amen.

A Solid Foundation

"Therefore everyone who hears these words of mine and puts them
into practice is like a wise man who built his house on the rock.
The rain came down, the streams rose, and the winds blew
and beat against that house; yet it did not fall,
because it had its foundation on the rock."
MATTHEW 7:24–25

God, Your Word won't lead me astray. I have anchored my life deep into the solid bedrock of Your teachings. And because my foundation will hold, I know that no matter what circumstance life chucks at me, my house will not fall. When the winds blow and my doctor tells me they've found cancer, my foundation still holds. When the rain splatters against the windowpanes and my boss says they have to let me go, my foundation holds. When the flood waters rise and my husband walks out, my foundation, the Rock of Ages who can't be moved, holds. Give me a steadfast spirit to cling to Your words through the dark storms. In Jesus' name, amen.

GROW ME UP

May he strengthen your hearts so that you will be blameless and holy in the presence of our God and Father when our Lord Jesus comes with all his holy ones.

1 THESSALONIANS 3:13

. . . .

Father, I don't need a self-help book or a motivating seminar. I need You to strengthen my heart so I can live a life of righteousness. I have You to supply the personal growth necessary for me to mature in my faith. It's not enough for me to say, "Oops, I'm sorry—again," each and every time I mess up. I need Your forgiveness, but with Your strength, I want to leave behind the wobbly legs of a newborn believer and run a competitive race where I'm not continually tripping over my own feet. Strengthen my heart so I can stand and overcome obstacles and make right decisions that please You. Lead me into a life of holiness. In Jesus' name, amen.

Second Chances

"I now establish my covenant with you and with your descendants after you and with every living creature that was with you—the birds, the livestock and all the wild animals, all those that came out of the ark with you—every living creature on earth. I establish my covenant with you: Never again will all life be destroyed by the waters of a flood; never again will there be a flood to destroy the earth."

Genesis 9:9–11

God, You didn't have to give us another chance. Your beautiful creation had been corrupted. Wickedness and evil were stomping the life out of goodness and love in the hearts of Your master-piece. How that must have grieved You, just as it pierces a mother to see her children hurting one another. You could have ended it all that day, swept away the brokenness with the decisive hand of a tsunami. But You didn't. Instead, You saved a family to begin again. And You made us a promise. But Your love was too great to stop there. Because You are a God of mercy and love, You sent us Your Son to repair the breach in our relationship once and for all—You sent us salvation. Amen.

A New Perspective

Consider it pure joy, my brothers and sisters, whenever you face trials of many kinds, because you know that the testing of your faith produces perseverance. Let perseverance finish its work so that you may be mature and complete, not lacking anything.

JAMES 1:2–4

Father, to some, bruised clouds leaning over the horizon are a total drag, the ruination of all their plans and the murderer of their good mood. But to others, the promise of rain brings the anticipation of a relaxing day with a hot cup of coffee and a good book, and after all, the flowers always bloom so vibrantly after a good drenching. When thunderheads gather, whether it's a problem with finances, bad news from a doctor, or a broken relationship, help me to check my perspective. Bring joy to my spirit even in the hard parts of life because I know that You are working to complete me. My trials are merely a momentary doorway that leads to the sweet-smelling blossom of maturity. Amen.

Unveiled Glory

But whenever someone turns to the Lord, the veil is taken away.
For the Lord is the Spirit, and wherever the Spirit of the Lord is,
there is freedom. So all of us who have had that veil removed
can see and reflect the glory of the Lord. And the Lord—
who is the Spirit—makes us more and more like
him as we are changed into his glorious image.
2 Corinthians 3:16–18 nlt

Lord, Moses received Your covenant and his face shone from having been in the presence of Your glory. He covered the brightness with a veil because the Israelites could not bear to look at the glory reflected there. But under the new covenant, we are born into grace, and the veil is gone. We are freed by the Holy Spirit to both see and reflect Your glory. Thank You, Jesus, that by believing in You, Your truth has been unveiled to me. I can read Your words and understanding dawns in my mind as the Holy Spirit teaches me and guides me. I am being changed into Your glorious image. Make me more like You, Jesus. Teach me to reflect Your glory into this dark world. Amen.

A New Heart

I will give you a new heart and put a new spirit in you; I will remove from you your heart of stone and give you a heart of flesh. And I will put my Spirit in you and move you to follow my decrees and be careful to keep my laws. Then you will live in the land I gave your ancestors; you will be my people, and I will be your God.

Ezekiel 36:26–28

Father, Pinocchio was a puppet carved from wood who wanted to become a real boy. I also desire real life. I want a living heart that's tender and responsive to Your urgings. Take away my heart hardened by stubbornness and pride. Alone, I can't quicken a new heart, but You are the changer of hearts. Soften my heart and fill me with Your Spirit. Without You, I'm a puppet to the world's pleasures. Much like Pinocchio, I'm easily deceived into thinking the false satisfaction of this earth will lead to something lasting. But Your Spirit has cut my strings and given me new life. I want to be called Yours. I want to carefully obey Your ways. In Jesus' name, amen.

One More Day

This is the day the LORD has made.
We will rejoice and be glad in it.
PSALM 118:24 NLT

God, the sky is just beginning to awaken with the first glow of dawn. The birds are already cheering the rising sun with happy songs. The mist floats low over the fields as the first crimson rays filter through the trees. It's a new day! Yesterday is a memory and tomorrow but a hope, but today is here and with it a fresh start. A brand-new beginning. Another chance to praise You and do Your work. I will leave the mistakes and difficulties of yesterday in the past. Thank You, Jesus, for giving me another day to live for You. I will rejoice in this day because You made it and gifted it to me. May I use every waking moment of it for Your glory. Amen.

FILLED WITH GOD

*I pray that you, being rooted and established in love, may have power,
together with all the Lord's holy people, to grasp how wide and long
and high and deep is the love of Christ, and to know this love
that surpasses knowledge—that you may be filled to
the measure of all the fullness of God.*

<small>EPHESIANS 3:17–19</small>

Lord, You think big! It wasn't enough for You to create the world and set it spinning. You also planned in intricate detail how You would save us and spend all of eternity with us. But even that wasn't enough for Your ultimate plan. You also left us with Your Spirit to help and teach us. Filled to the measure of all the fullness of God—I can hardly imagine what that should look like. The total package of Your love, mercy, goodness, joy, and peace dwell within me as Your Holy Spirit. When I'm lacking patience, at my call is the fullness of Your patience. When my mood is flagging, Your abundant joy resides within me. Allow me to experience Your fullness today. In Jesus' name, amen.

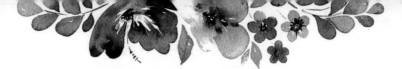

Increased Love

*May the Lord make your love increase and overflow for each
other and for everyone else, just as ours does for you.*
1 Thessalonians 3:12

Father, thank You that I don't have to remain as I am. You continually work to make me more like Jesus, and I can ask You for more of the things that I lack. I no longer have to believe the lie that "Oh, I'm just not an empathetic person," or "I'm not much of a servant." You can increase my love so that it rushes like a swollen creek in spring and overflows onto everyone around me. Increase my love today, Lord. Show me those who are in need of Your healing love and let me be Your hands and feet. Reveal the dams in my life that are blocking the flow of Your love—selfishness, pride, bitterness—and remove them. In Jesus' name, amen.

Ever-Present Help

God is our refuge and strength, an ever-present help in trouble.
Therefore we will not fear, though the earth give way and the
mountains fall into the heart of the sea, though its waters roar
and foam and the mountains quake with their surging. . . .
The LORD Almighty is with us; the God of Jacob is our fortress.
PSALM 46:1–3, 7

God, sometimes my emotions overtake me at the smallest hiccups in my day—I broke my favorite dish or my car runs out of gas. Here I am upset over the little stuff when You have promised to keep me through much bigger problems than my chipped nail polish or failed dinner attempt. You promise to be my refuge if the mountains fall into the heart of the sea. I can admit that even my worst day hasn't approached a disaster of that magnitude. And even if my mountains aren't quite quaking, You still care about my problems. You are my ever-present help in trouble. I can call on the Lord Almighty at any time—even if it's only over a broken dish. Amen.

PRODIGALS WELCOME

"The father said to his servants, 'Quick! Bring the best robe and put it on him. Put a ring on his finger and sandals on his feet. Bring the fattened calf and kill it. Let's have a feast and celebrate. For this son of mine was dead and is alive again; he was lost and is found.' So they began to celebrate."
LUKE 15:22–24

Lord, how often do we walk away from You? How often do we make choices that grieve Your Father's heart? Our leaving isn't always in big, rebellious ways. Instead, we turn aside by saying we'll pray later or we'll spend time in Your Word tomorrow when we're not so busy. I'll give a little more next month when my expenses aren't so great. I'll help when my time isn't so pressed. And yet Jesus said that the father saw his wayward son returning and ran out to meet him. Father, You rejoice over me when I return to You in repentance. You celebrate my contrite spirit with feasting and new robes. Thank You for seeing into my heart and wrapping Your welcoming arms around me. In Jesus' name, amen.

ALL THINGS NEW

You were taught, with regard to your former way of life, to put off your old self, which is being corrupted by its deceitful desires; to be made new in the attitude of your minds; and to put on the new self, created to be like God in true righteousness and holiness.

EPHESIANS 4:22–24

· ·

God, I was broken, defeated, wretched, and hopeless. I was burned out, but at my weakest point, Your strength was there. Your grace found me in my despair, and Your perfect love called me by name. I was dead, but You gave me life. You repaired my broken places, and my damaged heart began to beat again. You made me new. You revived me. And now I'm alive in You. Apart from You, there is nothing for me to place my hope in. Without You, everything is meaningless and bleak. I want to be new in You every day, to strip off the old, corrupted attitudes and habits that used to rule me, and live anew in righteousness and holiness. In Jesus' name, amen.

A WAY MAKER

This is what the LORD says—he who made a way through the sea,
a path through the mighty waters. . . ."Forget the former things;
do not dwell on the past. See, I am doing a new thing! Now it
springs up; do you not perceive it? I am making a way in
the wilderness and streams in the wasteland."
ISAIAH 43:16, 18–19

Lord, I've been lost in what seems like impossible circumstances. My anxiety builds as I turn every facet and examine every possibility only to find every avenue closed to me. There seems to be no escape. I feel like the Israelites, backs to the sea, facing an army of chariots. But then I remember that You made a way where there was none before. My mortal eyes may not perceive Your workings, but I know that You are the Way Maker. You rolled back the waves and the Israelites passed through to a new land. You can spring up streams in my wasteland and blaze a way through my wilderness. Meet me here in my desert and lead me home. In the name of Jesus, amen.

BEAUTY INSTEAD OF ASHES

The LORD has anointed me to proclaim good news to the poor.
He has sent me to bind up the brokenhearted, to proclaim freedom for
the captives and release from darkness for the prisoners, to proclaim
the year of the LORD's favor and the day of vengeance of our God, to
comfort all who mourn, and provide for those who grieve in Zion—
to bestow on them a crown of beauty instead of ashes.

ISAIAH 61:1–3

Lord, how can I not rejoice in the hope-filled message of Your good news? You sent us a Savior! You sent us a Healer to take our pain and fuse our brokenness back together. You sent us a Champion to break our chains and set the captives of darkness free into Your marvelous light. You gave us a better life and a new way to live. You sent us comfort and strength and hope. You brushed away the ashes of mourning from my head and placed a crown of beauty there instead. Imagine the excitement of some when Jesus stood in the temple that day and said, "It's Me! I'm the One you've been waiting for. I've been sent!" In Jesus' powerful name, amen.

COMPASSIONATE FATHER

*As a father has compassion on his children, so the LORD has
compassion on those who fear him; for he knows how
we are formed, he remembers that we are dust.*

PSALM 103:13–14

God, we come from humble beginnings. After You created man
from a pile of dust in the garden of Eden, You breathed the breath
of life into his being. Minus Your breath, we are but dead and life-
less dirt. Flawed as I am, I often struggle in habitual sin and missed
goals. Over and over I fall short of the mark. Sometimes I wonder
how You can continue to put up with my unkept promises and
faltering faith. But You remember my ultimate source—just dust.
And Your compassion abounds. You don't treat me as I deserve;
instead, You crown me with love and compassion and satisfy my
desires with good things (Psalm 103:4–5). Forgive my unfaithful
ways in the face of Your steadfast love. Amen.

He Never Gives Up

But our citizenship is in heaven. And we eagerly await a Savior from there, the Lord Jesus Christ, who, by the power that enables him to bring everything under his control, will transform our lowly bodies so that they will be like his glorious body.

Philippians 3:20–21

Father, soften the hard clay of my heart so that it is yielded to Your sculpting hand on my life. Help me to heed Your Holy Spirit's urgings. You are the Master Artist who would mold my heart into something beautiful if I surrender my will to Yours. I'm so grateful that You don't give up on me. Even when I falter and stray from You, You're capable of redeeming my poor choices and making me more like Jesus. I look ahead toward heaven, my true home, and the things of this world shift into proper perspective. They're temporary. They're shallow. They're distractions. Give me eyes that see and ears that hear as You continue to do the good work in me that You started. Amen.

He Does the Impossible

This is the confidence we have in approaching God
that if we ask anything according to his will, he hears us.
And if we know that he hears us—whatever we ask—
we know that we have what we asked of him.

1 John 5:14–15

God, sometimes I underestimate Your awesome power. I ask for things but don't really expect You to move. It seems impossible to change things. When the apostle Peter was in prison for preaching Your Gospel, the believers gathered in an all-night prayer vigil, and You showed up in a huge way. You sent an angel to release Peter from prison—dropped his chains and walked him right out the gate! Yet when Peter showed up at the house, the believers were shocked by his arrival. They expected so much less from You. Give me faith that when I pray according to Your will, You will answer in big ways. Shock me with Your power to bring about the seemingly impossible. In Jesus' name, amen.

THE REAL DEAL

"I am the LORD, and there is no other. I have not spoken in secret, from somewhere in a land of darkness; I have not said to Jacob's descendants, 'Seek me in vain.' I, the LORD, speak the truth. . . . Ignorant are those who carry about idols of wood, who pray to gods that cannot save. . . . Turn to me and be saved. . .for I am God, and there is no other."
Isaiah 45:18–20, 22

Lord, You are the God who created the heavens and fashioned the earth. There are no substitutes for You. And yet we humans have tried so hard for millennia to carve out our own forged gods. They're powerless, and yet we give them our attention and devotion as if they cared about us in return, as You do. You created this fantastic and beautiful planet especially for us, Your ultimate creation. You wanted a relationship with us so completely that You sent Your Son to die for us. Show me any weak substitutes I've replaced You with. Reveal the things I use for comfort and security instead of seeking You. I want more of You, God. You are the I Am. There is no other. Amen.

His Mercy Abounds

"Blessed are the merciful, for they will be shown mercy."
MATTHEW 5:7

God, Your limitless capacity for mercy astounds me. Jesus said during the Sermon on the Mount: "Blessed are the merciful, for they will be shown mercy." It's tempting to think that our mercy toward others somehow kindles Your mercy toward us. But Yours was first. While we were still sinners, You died for us. Jesus was trying to tell us that if we truly understand and accept the mercy that You graciously give, then we would have no option but to be merciful to all. After we've been forgiven a massive debt we could never in a million lifetimes repay, how could we offer less to others? Help me show my gratitude for Your mercy by giving it freely to everyone I encounter. Amen.

A New Batch

Don't you know that a little yeast leavens the whole batch of dough?
Get rid of the old yeast, so that you may be a new unleavened
batch—as you really are. For Christ, our Passover lamb, has been
sacrificed. Therefore let us keep the Festival, not with the old
bread leavened with malice and wickedness, but with
the unleavened bread of sincerity and truth.

1 Corinthians 5:6–8

Lord, I can throw out my old habits like last week's smelly left-overs. It's so freeing to realize that I don't have to keep doing the same things I've always done, repeating mistakes and living with regrets. I'm not sentenced to a static lifestyle of self-destructive sin. Instead, You've called me out of it. I'm a new batch of bread, as I was always meant to be. Now I can live a sincere life of truth, minus the yeast of sin. You've shown me how a little sin can ruin my entire life. Now help me to do like the Israelites before Passover and sweep every speck of yeast from my house. Show me anything in my life that isn't pleasing to You. Amen.

He Restores

The LORD is my shepherd, I lack nothing. He makes me lie down in green pastures, he leads me beside quiet waters, he refreshes my soul.
PSALM 23:1–3

. . . .

Lord, I'm tired, worn out, and beat down. I'm exhausted from fighting the same old battles every day. I'm emotionally on edge and about to graduate to hot mess. I'm not sure I can stay in this war another day. But I know that You give strength to the weary and rest to the burdened. You are a compassionate and tender God who cares for me. Instead of losing patience with my toddler-worthy tired attitude, You lovingly lead me to the rest and restoration that I need. You restore me to strength and refresh my perspective. Thank You for providing for all my needs—both physical and spiritual. Show me how to deal kindly toward others when they need refreshment. In the name of Jesus, amen.

No Equal

"To whom will you compare me? Or who is my equal?" says the Holy One. Lift up your eyes and look to the heavens: Who created all these? He who brings out the starry host one by one and calls forth each of them by name. Because of his great power and mighty strength, not one of them is missing.

ISAIAH 40:25–26

. . . .

God, why do I bother with fear when You are bigger than the vastness of our ever-expanding universe? You have no equal! I slip out at night under a blanket of countless stars and bask in the knowledge that You placed each one there. How great is the One who could name each and every twinkling sparkle in the black-velvet sky. You contain and surround all, and You hold everything together. I rest safely in the palm of Your powerful and mighty hand. My life is clutched in Your grasp and guided by Your will. Wipe away my fears and replace them with faith and trust. Make my life yielded to the movement of Your will. In the name of Jesus, amen.

LIVING BREAD

"I am the bread of life. Your ancestors ate the manna in the wilderness, yet they died. But here is the bread that comes down from heaven, which anyone may eat and not die. I am the living bread that came down from heaven. Whoever eats this bread will live forever. This bread is my flesh, which I will give for the life of the world."
JOHN 6:48–51

Father, we eat our fill and satisfy our hunger only to hear our stomachs grumble for more in a few short hours. Our physical bodies burn through food and crave more, always more. Spiritually, we have the same insatiable appetite. I've tried to satisfy it with the junk food of society. I've consumed the world's buffet of living for myself, being good, obtaining money, but after a while I feel empty again. But You, Jesus, are the Bread of Life. Living bread that fills all my voids and never leaves me hungry. Since I've found You, I don't need to return again and again to the world's table, looking for that something to satisfy me. In You I have found what my soul craves. Amen.

He Will Be There

*"Be strong and courageous. Do not be afraid or terrified because of them, for the L*ORD *your God goes with you; he will never leave you nor forsake you."*

DEUTERONOMY 31:6

. . . .

Lord, when the sparkle dims and my walls begin to crumble, then I find out who will truly be there for me when it all falls apart. When I can't sink any further, whether from my own making or circumstances beyond my control, often people will forget me or abandon me in my downward plunge. But You, Lord, have promised never to leave me or forsake me. Even if life forces me to what feels like the deepest ocean trench, You will be there. You will give me the courage I need. You will prove faithful because it's not in Your character to falter. I have no fear, because my God will always go with me. In the steadfast name of Jesus, amen.

PURSUED

For day and night your hand was heavy on me; my strength was sapped as in the heat of summer. Then I acknowledged my sin to you and did not cover up my iniquity. I said, "I will confess my transgressions to the LORD. And you forgave the guilt of my sin."

PSALM 32:4–5

Lord, King David tried to cover up his sin, but that only led to more sin. And You didn't let him get away with it. He probably should have known that hiding was futile. People might not discover what he'd done, but You see right into our hearts and know all. When I do wrong, my natural inclination is also to pull a cover-up job. But You love me too much to let me slide into sin unhindered. Like the dense weight of the summer heat, when walking out of my air-conditioning feels like smacking into concrete, Your hand of conviction presses upon me until I tire of running and turn to You. And when I confess, I experience the cool relief of Your forgiveness. Amen.

His Own Possession

For the grace of God has appeared that offers salvation to all people. It teaches us to say "No" to ungodliness and worldly passions, and to live self-controlled, upright and godly lives in this present age, while we wait for the blessed hope—the appearing of the glory of our great God and Savior, Jesus Christ, who gave himself for us to redeem us from all wickedness and to purify for himself a people that are his very own, eager to do what is good.

Titus 2:11–14

Lord, Your grace has come to earth. All those years ago, You stepped down out of glory to usher in the age of grace. You were born as a helpless baby to bring salvation to all people—including me. And now we wait for Your glorious appearing because You purified us to be Your own special possession. You've trained me to live a new life, to abandon the practices of the world, and to live upright and godly in the midst of this sinful age. I now belong to You. Instead of always looking out for myself, I'm now eager to help others. My priorities seem odd to those who don't know You, but I pray my lifestyle will lead them into Your great grace. Amen.

My Champion

"You have seen with your own eyes all that the LORD your God has done to these two kings. The LORD will do the same to all the kingdoms over there where you are going. Do not be afraid of them; the LORD your God himself will fight for you."

DEUTERONOMY 3:21–22

· ·

Lord, I know You've got my back when I'm walking in Your will. You promised to fight the Israelites' battles for them if they would obey You and trust in Your promises. You'll fight mine too if I step out in faith in the direction You're nudging me. After all, if You are for me, who can be against me? No one can stand against the mighty God of creation who holds all power and knowledge in the palm of His hand. Give me faith to go where You lead and see what You will do. You have brought down city walls and sent enemy armies fleeing in terror. I don't have to fear when You are the champion of my cause. In Jesus' name, amen.

POWER

But I will come to you very soon, if the Lord is willing, and then I will find out not only how these arrogant people are talking, but what power they have. For the kingdom of God is not a matter of talk but of power.

1 CORINTHIANS 4:19–20

. . . .

Lord, we're big fans of talk. We have talk shows and sports commentators and seminars for every subject under the sun. But too often our talk isn't backed up by anything substantial. They say talk is cheap for a reason. Because it is. Talk has no power, no movement, no achievement. It's just words until someone gets up and does something. But Your kingdom, Father, is no matter of mere talk. Your kingdom is about power—the power of living a changed life. The power of new birth that reveals itself in a life fully on task for Your mission. The power of becoming a humble servant for Jesus. It's the power of change, the power of true life. Amen.

Perfect Love

As we live in God, our love grows more perfect. So we will not be afraid on the day of judgment, but we can face him with confidence because we live like Jesus here in this world. Such love has no fear, because perfect love expels all fear. If we are afraid, it is for fear of punishment, and this shows that we have not fully experienced his perfect love.
1 John 4:17–18 NLT

Lord, my life before You was stamped with anxiety and fear. I was afraid that there was no recovering from all the mistakes I had already made, that they would bury me in an avalanche of condemnation. I pictured Your wrath and stern frown with each new blot on my record. I couldn't seem to stop doing the wrong thing and wondered how many rights it would take to blot out a wrong. But then I discovered that only the blood of Jesus could wash away my wrongs. I found Your love that expels all fear. Now I have confidence in my forgiveness. I have experienced the relief of Your perfect love and my fears fled. In the name of Jesus, amen.

GIVER OF WISDOM

*If any of you lacks wisdom, you should ask God, who gives generously
to all without finding fault, and it will be given to you.*
JAMES 1:5

God, how often have I wondered and worried about what to do,
which choice was the right one? Or if a path even exists that leads
through my knotted mess. I've fretted and wrung my hands and
probably gained more than a few gray hairs agonizing over what
I should say or do—or not do. And all that anxious energy I've
expended wearing out my floorboards at midnight is a complete
waste. I spark no insight from the deaf walls huddled around me.
But all I need to do is ask You. You won't criticize or reprimand me
for my questions. Instead, You will give Your advice generously.
Father, I need Your wisdom. Show me what to do. In Jesus' name,
amen.

PATH TO ETERNITY

"Blessed are the poor in spirit, for theirs is the kingdom of heaven. Blessed are those who mourn, for they will be comforted. Blessed are the meek, for they will inherit the earth. Blessed are those who hunger and thirst for righteousness, for they will be filled."
MATTHEW 5:3–6

God, our future is full of hope—the promise of an eternal place of peace with You. Thank You, Jesus, for pointing us toward the road that leads to heaven. Thank You for walking up a mountain-side and sitting down to teach the masses how to live in Your kingdom. You said we're blessed when we recognize our spiritual bankruptcy before a holy God. You promised to comfort those who grieve over the sins they have committed against You. And those who clearly recognize their humble position will inherit everything. When we realize our great need for You and hunger and thirst to know more of You, You will satisfy us with the bread of life and living water. In the name of Jesus, amen.

Remembered No More

*"For I will forgive their wickedness and
will remember their sins no more."*
JEREMIAH 31:34

Lord, we often say we'll forgive and forget, but sometimes I find myself dwelling on wrongs done to me that I thought I'd forgiven. I thought I'd put it behind me and laid it to rest, but then the old hurt pops into my mind again and I feel resentment stirring in my heart. Then I have to cycle through releasing it to You—again. But when You forgive, You don't remember my sins anymore. You will never allow them to come between us again. You don't remind me of how I messed up before or throw them in my face. Help me let go of the offenses others have committed against me as completely as You have let go of mine. Keep my relationships unclouded by bitterness. Amen.

Tender Shepherd

Jesus went through all the towns and villages, teaching in their synagogues, proclaiming the good news of the kingdom and healing every disease and sickness. When he saw the crowds, he had compassion on them, because they were harassed and helpless, like sheep without a shepherd.

Matthew 9:35–36

Father, sometimes I entertain the wrong image of You. I think that You condemn me, that You're waiting for me to mess up so You can punish me for each and every failure. That I have to be perfect in order to be accepted by You. But I don't have to put on my Sunday clothes for You. I couldn't even if I tried. You don't look upon me with censure and anger and impatience as I stumble along after You, You see me with eyes of compassion. You know that I'm harassed and helpless, a lamb in need of a strong and caring shepherd. Thank You, Jesus, for Your compassionate care of me. You have guided me into healing and abundant life in Your kingdom. Amen.

He Sees You

Why do you say, Israel, "My way is hidden from the L<small>ORD</small>; my cause is disregarded by my God"? Do you not know? Have you not heard? The L<small>ORD</small> is the everlasting God, the Creator of the ends of the earth. He will not grow tired or weary, and his understanding no one can fathom.

<small>ISAIAH 40:27–28</small>

God, I'm struggling right now. I'm feeling vulnerable and invisible. My strength is waning and I'm not sure I can go on like this. Do You see me? Look at this mess. Where is my help? I'm tired. Have You forgotten me here? No. I know that You haven't. My ways are not hidden from Your sight. You shield the weak and heavy-laden of Your flock, and You are gentle with me when I need special care. Open my eyes to the ways You are caring for me even now. You know my needs and give me just the right amount of strength to get through my difficulty. I am never alone. Your eye is always on me. Forgive me for complaining instead of trusting. Amen.

EQUIPPED

For we are God's handiwork, created in Christ Jesus to do good works, which God prepared in advance for us to do.

EPHESIANS 2:10

Lord, when You call me to do something for Your kingdom, You don't leave me hanging to figure it out on my own. When You call me, You equip me, You enable me, You provide for me. You outfit me specifically for the task You've called me to do, like one would a frontiersman preparing to trek into the wilderness. You give me the strength and the ability for the work I'm doing. You love me so enormously that You wouldn't send me in ill-equipped. Help me trust Your preparations and actively ready myself to be an effective tool in Your hand. In Jesus' name, amen.

Promise Keeper

God is not human, that he should lie, not a human being,
that he should change his mind. Does he speak and
then not act? Does he promise and not fulfill?
NUMBERS 23:19

God, I'm ashamed to say that I've made empty promises before. Whether I fully intended to keep my word and then got distracted from my purpose or knew that I most likely wouldn't follow through, it's still a broken promise. I'm guilty of changing my mind, failing to act when I should, and forgetting at times. Unlike me, God, You always keep Your word and never change Your mind. Your promises are brimming with hope because I know that they aren't empty platitudes. The full weight of Your divine personality backs them up. You always do what You say You will. Where I have failed to meet the standard, You are the ultimate Promise Keeper. In the name of Jesus, amen.

A Sure Thing

For this God is our God for ever and ever;
he will be our guide even to the end.
PSALM 48:14

God, it seems the only sure thing in this life is change—beginnings and endings, transitions, movement and turning, progress, rising and falling. I reach a comfortable place only to open a new door and close an old one. But there is one sure thing in my life that I can always count on—You. You are the Alpha and the Omega, the beginning and the end, the first and the last. You have always been and always will be. My mind doesn't stretch into that time zone of eternity, but it brings me great comfort to know that I serve an ageless God who will guide me to the end. And my end on earth is but another beginning, a doorway into eternity. Amen.

MY BURDEN BEARER

Praise be to the Lord, to God our Savior,
who daily bears our burdens. Our God is a God who saves.
PSALM 68:19–20

Father, I've got baggage. As I've walked through years here, I've picked up a little hurt there, a bit of anger here, a dose of pain and heartbreak, some struggles and insecurity. The weight of it curls over my shoulders and drags my steps. It dampens my joy and steals my laughter. But You are the Burden Bearer. Your Word says that You will daily bear my burdens. Father, Your shoulders are broad and strong, and I feel oh so weak right now. I'm handing over my stuff. Take it and rejuvenate my joy in a Savior who is able to carry my load. Thank You, Father, for Your compassion! My soul feels so much lighter now that You've relieved me. In Jesus' name, amen.

FIRM FOOTING

My help comes from the LORD, the Maker of heaven
and earth. He will not let your foot slip—he who
watches over you will not slumber.
PSALM 121:2–3

God, I know that shaky feeling as I'm walking along a trail and I suddenly lose traction. I've stepped in mud or on a mossy rock and my arms windmill as my stomach somersaults because I know I'm going down hard. But a friend reaches out and grabs my hand to steady me, and I find my footing once again. My galloping heart slows as I realize I've been delivered from a nasty fall. When I follow You and walk along my faith journey living in Your will, You promise not to let my foot slip. You steady me and show me where there's solid ground to tread on. You watch over me constantly. I never have to worry that You'll be napping during my crisis. Amen.

Unshakable

*I keep my eyes always on the LORD. With him at my right hand,
I will not be shaken. Therefore my heart is glad and my tongue rejoices.
. . . You make known to me the path of life; you will fill me with joy
in your presence, with eternal pleasures at your right hand.*

PSALM 16:8–9, 11

Lord, I love living in Your presence. When I wander from Your side and become distracted by the offerings of this world, I lose my peace and joy and my sense of purpose. I begin to wonder, *What's the point of all this struggle?* But when my eyes are on You, I am unshakable. Joy explodes within me and my purpose here is crystal clear. Without You, I have no reason. Without You, nothing makes sense and life is meaningless. But with You, God, I know that this world is but a prelude to my real life in eternity with You. And oh, what joys and unimaginable pleasure I will experience when I meet You face-to-face. In Jesus' name, amen.

DEFENDER OF THE HELPLESS

You, LORD, hear the desire of the afflicted; you encourage them, and you listen to their cry, defending the fatherless and the oppressed, so that mere earthly mortals will never again strike terror.
PSALM 10:17–18

Heavenly Father, when I am helpless and struggling, when I feel as if the waters of life are closing over my head, You hear my hopes and my desires. Your ears are attuned to my pained cry. You defend the oppressed, the weak, the marginalized, the unwanted. The undesirables of this world belong to You—You claimed them as Your heirs. You offer encouragement when I need it and soothe my fears. Jesus, You said that You didn't come to earth for the proud righteous, but for the bedraggled sinners who recognize their hopelessly wretched condition without You. I'm one of Your misfits, transformed by mercy into a marvelous new creation. Thank You, Father, for defending me in my vulnerability. In the name of Jesus, amen.

Towering Rock of Safety

*O God, listen to my cry! Hear my prayer! From the ends of the earth,
I cry to you for help when my heart is overwhelmed. Lead me to the
towering rock of safety, for you are my safe refuge, a fortress
where my enemies cannot reach me. Let me live forever in
your sanctuary, safe beneath the shelter of your wings!*
PSALM 61:1–4 NLT

God, how many seasons have I spent floundering in an overwhelmed state? Worries and responsibilities crash over me. My heart cries, "It's too much!" It's so encouraging to read King David's words, a man after Your own heart, who struggled like I do. And yet here I find the wellspring of his fearlessness and peace—he lived in Your sanctuary. Amid the war and turmoil of his life, he found a place of rest and safety in You. God, lead me to Your towering rock of safety, for You are my safe refuge. I want to discover unshakable rest and tranquil peace of mind forever in Your sanctuary, a place far from the grasping claws of my anxiety. In the name of Jesus, amen.

Remember All His Benefits

Praise the LORD, my soul, and forget not all his benefits—who forgives all your sins and heals all your diseases, who redeems your life from the pit and crowns you with love and compassion, who satisfies your desires with good things so that your youth is renewed like the eagle's.

PSALM 103:2–5

. . . .

Lord, we celebrate Mother's Day to honor and appreciate our moms and Father's Day for our dads. We celebrate Memorial Day to remember our veterans and soldiers, but how often do we celebrate just to remember all You have done for us? Do I dwell often enough on Your benefits? Lifting my depressed spirits should be as easy as remembering the numerous blessings You have bestowed on me and all Your people through the ages. I sit in church on Sunday and dwell on my anxiety and prioritize my to-do list when I should be remembering just how blessed You have made me. Help me make each Sunday and every day in between a day of remembrance, a day of counting blessings. In Jesus' name, amen.

MY FLASHLIGHT

Your word is a lamp for my feet, a light on my path.
PSALM 119:105

God, traveling at night can be nerve-racking. I get a little nervous when the darkness closes in around me, especially on back roads beyond the reach of streetlights, where little moonlight filters through the trees. My headlights glow like a beacon, illuminating the path in front of me. But what if they went out? I would be hopelessly lost and unable to see curves or dangers in the road. Thank You, God, for giving me a light for my travels through life. Your Word lights up the right path when I'm confused and comforts me when my darkest fears seem imminent. It guides me toward You like a lighthouse leading a ship safely into its home harbor. In the name of Jesus, amen.

He's Greater

You, dear children, are from God and have overcome them,
because the one who is in you is greater than
the one who is in the world.

1 John 4:4

Father, I perch on the edge of my seat at sporting events, waiting and watching to see who will prevail. Hoping that my team will pull through for the victory. How wonderful it is as a believer in You to already be assured that I'm part of the winning team. You are greater than the one who is in this world! You've already won the victory. Your reign as champion is secure. And because I'm one of Your children, I too am undefeated. Satan may try to convince me that I'm nobody and a hopeless failure, but all I need to do is remember that You're greater. Greater than my failures. Greater than my fears. Greater than my hurts. And I belong to You. Amen.

Perfect Peace

You will keep in perfect peace those whose minds are
steadfast, because they trust in you. Trust in the Lord
forever, for the Lord, *the* Lord *himself, is the Rock eternal.*
Isaiah 26:3–4

God, where else could I go to receive perfect peace? Many sources claim to give peace of mind, but who can truly give it but You? I desperately need Your peace today, God. My mind is troubled with worries, to-do lists, regrets, and guilt. I need You to whisper, "Be still," into the churning waters of my soul. Soothe my stress-filled emotions and give me rest as I focus my thoughts on You. Your Word says that You will keep in perfect peace those whose minds are steadfast, because they trust in You. I trust You, God. I trust in Your goodness and mercy. I will firmly fix my eyes on You amid the disturbing distractions of life and feel Your perfect peace wash over me. Amen.

Heart's Desire

Don't worry about the wicked or envy those who do wrong. For like grass, they soon fade away. Like spring flowers, they soon wither. Trust in the LORD and do good. Then you will live safely in the land and prosper. Take delight in the LORD, and he will give you your heart's desires.

PSALM 37:1–4 NLT

. . . .

Father, I can trust in Your provision because You always have my best interests at heart. Even when I at times, like a young child naive to potential harm, want things that aren't good for me. Those who live for themselves instead of You sometimes seem to be flourishing while I struggle to follow You. But all I have to do is look to my eternal future to find encouragement. My daffodils are glorious in early May, but their reign of beauty in my garden is fleeting. Soon their petals turn brown and crumble. The wicked will wither and fade like spring flowers. I will trust You and follow You, and You will fulfill all of my deepest longings. In Jesus' name, amen.

CARRIED AWAY

As far as the east is from the west,
so far has he removed our transgressions from us.
PSALM 103:12

God, Your forgiving nature shocks me. I've been guilty of envisioning You as harsh and unyielding, but the essence of Your nature is gracious and welcoming. You don't want to punish us; instead Your love, mercy, grace, and kindness lead to Your desire to forgive us and welcome us freely. When You forgive me, You carry my sins far away from me and cover them with Your blood. David said as far as the east is from the west—an immeasurable distance. We cannot determine where west gives way to east. My guilt no longer ravages my soul because the stains are washed away. Your forgiveness is the best news we guilty humans could ever receive. In Jesus' name, amen.

Still Yours

*My heart was bitter, and I was all torn up inside. I was so foolish
and ignorant. . . . Yet I still belong to you; you hold my right hand.
You guide me with your counsel, leading me to a glorious destiny.
Whom have I in heaven but you? I desire you more than anything
on earth. My health may fail, and my spirit may grow weak,
but God remains the strength of my heart; he is mine forever.*

PSALM 73:21–26 NLT

God, I'm so glad that even after I've been a fool, after I've envied
the accomplishments and wealth and seeming ease of those who
don't follow You, that I still belong to You. Show me how much
more You have waiting for me in the glorious eternity You're preparing than the shallow and unfulfilling treasures of this world.
When I spend time with You and read Your scriptures, I see things
more clearly. Those who don't love You may prosper for a short
time, but ultimately will fall into ruin. Make the prayer of my heart
always be that I would desire You more than anything I find here
on earth. You are all I need. In Jesus' name, amen.

GOD OF THE LIVING

"But about the resurrection of the dead—have you not read what God said to you, 'I am the God of Abraham, the God of Isaac, and the God of Jacob'? He is not the God of the dead but of the living."

MATTHEW 22:31–32

. . . .

Father God, before I knew You I was dead. I wandered aimlessly through my life, drifting with selfish ambition as my only guide. I was enslaved by my desires and blind to Your purpose for my life. But You found me, Jesus. You showed me a better way, and now I am alive! I've been revived! I have awakened to Your plans for my life, and I no longer feel meaningless. It's as if a blindfold has fallen from my eyes and suddenly I see You everywhere. The work of Your hands surrounds me. I see You in Your creation in a child's laugh, and even in my pain. I have found new meaning in living for You. In the name of Jesus, amen.

UNSHAKABLE LOVE

"Though the mountains be shaken and the hills be removed,
yet my unfailing love for you will not be shaken nor my covenant of
peace be removed," says the LORD, who has compassion on you.
ISAIAH 54:10

. . . .

Lord, mountains have roots that are sunk deep into the earth. It takes a colossal force of nature or explosives to give one even a little shiver. I look out over the rolling hills and wonder how it would be possible to remove them from the landscape. These sturdy land formations seem so permanent. And yet You promise that Your love for me and Your covenant of peace are more deeply entrenched than the mountains and the hills. Your love is unfailing—never to be removed or shaken. Nothing I do could make You stop loving me. You love me with a love that's rooted deeper than the mountains because You chose to, because I am Yours. In Jesus' name, amen.

My Advisor

I will bless the LORD who guides me; even at night my heart instructs me. I know the LORD is always with me. I will not be shaken, for he is right beside me.

PSALM 16:7–8 NLT

. . . .

God, I don't ever have to feel lost again, because You are my ever-present guide. Even during the dark nights of uncertainty and worry, You are my advisor. You're always willing to lead me with Your wisdom if I will only listen to Your instruction. But sometimes I seek other, less reliable, means of guidance and I end up in a mess. Help me to come to You first. Give me eyes to see and ears to hear Your instructions—and a willing heart to obey. Forgive me for the times I've chosen disobedience to You. You are a patient and compassionate teacher. Give me wisdom, and keep my feet on the path that leads to Your blessing. In the name of Jesus, amen.

Safe in His Hand

"But ask the animals, and they will teach you, or the birds in the sky, and they will tell you; or speak to the earth, and it will teach you, or let the fish in the sea inform you. Which of all these does not know that the hand of the LORD has done this? In his hand is the life of every creature and the breath of all mankind."

JOB 12:7–10

Father, at times my life seems so small and fragile in this world of unpredictability and scary circumstances. Who can say what will happen in the next moment? But I can put my anxiety at ease because I rest in Your hand. I am vulnerable and weak, but nothing can take me out of Your palm. That doesn't mean that hard things will never come to me, but I know that when they do, You will be there with me. You will lend me Your strength and make sure I have everything I need to come through my trials in Your power. When I am weak, You are strong. Your power works most effectively in my weakness. I am held and comforted by You. Amen.

PRECIOUS PAIN

My suffering was good for me, for it taught me to pay attention to your decrees. Your instructions are more valuable to me than millions in gold and silver.

PSALM 119:71–72 NLT

Lord, I don't often thank You for the times that I suffer or the hardships I encounter. I tend to see them as something to be avoided and beg You to deliver me from them as fast as possible instead of recognizing them as opportunities to learn more about You. You shape me through the fires I endure by removing the impurities in my character. Your loving hand shaves off the excess. Thank You for redeeming even my failures and turning them into my greatest victories. Your lessons are precious to me. Show me how You want to change me through my trials. All the money in the world cannot equal the unfathomable worth of becoming more like Jesus. In Jesus' name, amen.

Remarkable Secrets

*"This is what the LORD says—the LORD who made the earth,
who formed and established it, whose name is the LORD: Ask me and I
will tell you remarkable secrets you do not know about things to come."*
JEREMIAH 33:2–3 NLT

God, I see people around me chasing after fleeting pleasures and finding empty satisfaction in the comforts of this world. They ignore You and Your plan and think that this life is a race to have as much fun as they can before they die. But since I've come to know You, it's as if You've shared a secret with me. You've shown me what living really means and given me a sneak peek into the marvelous things You have in store for me both now and when I pass through the veil into eternity. Knowing even just a hint of Your amazing plan strengthens my faith and my decision to follow Your ways. Tell me more of Your secrets, God. In the name of Jesus, amen.

MY SHAME ERASED

*For God so loved the world that he gave his one and only Son,
that whoever believes in him shall not perish but have
eternal life. For God did not send his Son into the world to
condemn the world, but to save the world through him.
Whoever believes in him is not condemned.*

JOHN 3:16–18

God, You sent Jesus to us to bring life, not condemnation, to a world
hopelessly chained in sin. I have stood before You, head lowered in
shame for my actions—just like the woman the Pharisees dragged
before You. She'd been caught in the very act of sin, and they were
ready to stone her for her mistakes. But not You, Jesus. You sent
them away and said, "Has no one condemned you? . . . Neither do
I condemn you. Go now and leave your life of sin" (John 8:10-11).
Help me deal with others in love and not condemnation. Show me
how to speak the hope of new life in You to them and not to cast
stones in accusation and judgment. In Jesus' name, amen.

Joy Giver

Don't keep looking at my sins. Remove the stain of my guilt.
Create in me a clean heart, O God. Renew a loyal spirit within me.
Do not banish me from your presence, and don't take your Holy
Spirit from me. Restore to me the joy of your salvation,
and make me willing to obey you.

PSALM 51:9–12 NLT

Heavenly Father, I'm so grateful that when I mess up, I can come to You with a contrite heart. I'm a flawed human, and the will to follow Your ways fully doesn't reside in me. I need Your help. I can't do it alone. Give me a clean heart that is loyal only to You, God. Scour the ugly stain of guilt from my heart. Give me a spirit that's willing to obey You. Somehow, I thought for a moment that the things of earth would be more satisfying than obedience to You. I slipped, and I tried living for myself. But when I remember how You saved me, I'm overwhelmed with the joy of walking with You and the world's enticements fade. In Jesus' name, amen.

GOD'S YES!

No matter how many promises God has made, they are "Yes" in Christ. And so through him the "Amen" is spoken by us to the glory of God. Now it is God who makes both us and you stand firm in Christ. He anointed us, set his seal of ownership on us, and put his Spirit in our hearts as a deposit, guaranteeing what is to come.

2 CORINTHIANS 1:20–22

God, I'm so accustomed to hearing the disappointing word *no*. I even say it all the time to my children: "No, no, no, you may not do that or have that." But Your answer to me through Jesus is yes! Yes, I am a daughter in Christ. Yes, I can stand firm and leave my life of sin. Yes, I do have new life. Yes, I can have joy. Yes, I am empowered by Your Spirit and sealed as Yours. Yes, I will inherit eternal life. Your Holy Spirit is our guarantee that all Your promises will come true. Not a word You have uttered will be left unfulfilled. Thank You, God, for Your yes! In the name of Jesus, amen.

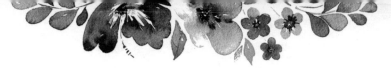

QUIET IN LOVE

*The Lord your God is in the midst of you, a Mighty One, a Savior
[Who saves]! He will rejoice over you with joy; He will rest
[in silent satisfaction] and in His love He will be silent and
make no mention [of past sins, or even recall them].*
ZEPHANIAH 3:17 AMPC

· ·

Father, silence can truly be golden. I have revisited the ways people
have hurt me or wronged me. Or I've dwelled in guilt over my own
mistakes. But I need to follow Your example and be silent and not
mention past sins or even recall them. What a blessing of Your great
grace that You aren't stewing over my mistakes. So neither should
I. I can repent and move forward. Help me deal in grace. Reveal to
me anyone I hold bitterness or unforgiveness toward. Help me let
go and be silent instead of lingering in a negative thought life. You
pick me up when I stumble and encourage me onward instead of
reminding me of all the times I've fallen. Amen.

Heiress

Day by day the LORD takes care of the innocent,
and they will receive an inheritance that lasts forever.
PSALM 37:18 NLT

God, You see into my heart and peer into the deepest fathoms of my soul. You know that I am far from innocent. I've messed up and made mistake after repeated mistake. But You also see the intent of my heart. You know that I love You and mourn the pain my sins have caused You. I want to please You and do good for You, even when I sometimes choose the wrong path. And because of Jesus' sacrifice, I can repent and be washed innocent again in Your eyes. You care for Your own. You've prepared an eternal inheritance just for me. I can hardly believe it! I may be poor on this earth, but I'm an heir to my Father's great fortune in heaven. Amen.

He Sees Me

"Were not the Cushites and Libyans a mighty army with great numbers of chariots and horsemen? Yet when you relied on the Lord, he delivered them into your hand. For the eyes of the Lord range throughout the earth to strengthen those whose hearts are fully committed to him."

2 Chronicles 16:8–9

Lord, You're not blind to my struggles. And I'm not following You in vain. Satan tries to convince me that You've left me to flounder when hardship or illness or broken relationships shatter my peace. He whispers, "Where is your God now?" But I know that You see me. Your eyes search the earth for Your faithful. You see my heart and know that I'm committed to You. Just as You gave manna to the Israelites to sustain them in the desert, You give me just the right amount of strength to persevere. Not so much that I think I'm doing it all on my own, but just enough so that I know it's You holding me. In the name of Jesus, amen.

Ask, Seek, Knock

"Ask and it will be given to you; seek and you will find; knock and the door will be opened to you. For everyone who asks receives; the one who seeks finds; and to the one who knocks, the door will be opened."
MATTHEW 7:7–8

God, what a fantastic promise! You're not holding anything back from me. But You do want some action on my part. Ask for forgiveness and You will give it to me. Seek after You and I will find and know the great living God. Knock on heaven's door and eternity will be opened before me. It seems too good to be true that a God as amazing as You would commit Yourself to me so fully—without reservations. I want to be that committed to You, God. I want You as my one and only. I want to search after You with single-minded focus so that I can find out all there is to know about You and Your ways. In Jesus' name, amen.

COUNTING TEARS

You keep track of all my sorrows. You have collected all my tears in your bottle. You have recorded each one in your book. My enemies will retreat when I call to you for help. This I know: God is on my side! I praise God for what he has promised; yes, I praise the LORD for what he has promised.
PSALM 56:8–10 NLT

God, You aren't indifferent to my pain. When sorrows like flaming arrows from the enemy seem to attack from every side, I know that You are keeping track of each and every hurt I suffer. You are measuring my tears and recording each teardrop in Your records. Because of Your great and unmatched love for me, You will pay back the enemy of my soul for all his wicked intentions toward me when the time is right. He will be destroyed, and I will receive Your promises. As I endure the momentary discomfort of this world, I can feel Your gentle hands cupping my cheeks as You say, "Just a little longer, My child. Rest while I fight for you. I have already vanquished this enemy." Amen.

STAY WITH GOD

I'm sure now I'll see God's goodness in the exuberant earth. Stay with GOD! *Take heart. Don't quit. I'll say it again: Stay with* GOD.
PSALM 27:13–14 MSG

God, I'm going to stick with You through this winding trek of life. I'm not going to quit even when I don't understand what You're doing. I'm going to trust. I'm going to wait for You. I see Your goodness all around me. It's evident in the crimson fingers streaking the dawn sky. It dances with the laughter of a child. It pours out with the quenching spring rain and the bright blossoms of May flowers. I see it in a stranger's smile. I feel it in the love I have for my family. You are a good Father. I will keep eternity in sight as my motivation to keep living for You, to keep doing the right thing until the end of my days here. Amen.

No Mere Mortal

For I am God and not a mere mortal.
I am the Holy One living among you.
HOSEA 11:9 NLT

. . . .

God, I'm in awe. You are the Holy One, the God who spoke an entire world into existence and puffed a breath of life into the nostrils of humankind. The power of Your voice alone changed reality and shifted things into existence that weren't there before. You speak and a creative force of will rocks the universe. You have chosen to live among us. Not a mere mortal, but the God of heaven and earth. The beginning of all things and the end of all things, You are an eternal being who was and is and will always be. And You're here with me. You've chosen me and loved me. In protection, You crouch over me, Lion of Judah, and roar at the enemy "Mine!" Amen.

Precious to Him

Long ago the LORD said to Israel: "I have loved you, my people, with
an everlasting love. With unfailing love I have drawn you to myself.
I will rebuild you, my virgin Israel. You will again be happy
and dance merrily with your tambourines."
JEREMIAH 31:3–4 NLT

Father, show me how You see me. I have allowed negative thought processes and self-criticism to distort Your opinion of me. Sometimes when I picture Your face, it's frowning in judgment. I know the enemy is putting lies in my head, because Your Word says there's no condemnation for Your children. And I am Your precious daughter. You love me with an everlasting love and have drawn me to You. You are pleased with me, Father, delighted to have me as Your child. You want happiness and goodness for my life, not suffering and turmoil. Reveal the lies I've been believing about You and teach me the truth You want me to know about Your unfailing love for me. In the name of Jesus, amen.

PURE PROMISES

Into the hovels of the poor, into the dark streets where the homeless groan, God speaks: "I've had enough; I'm on my way to heal the ache in the heart of the wretched." God's words are pure words, pure silver words refined seven times in the fires of his word-kiln, pure on earth as well as in heaven. GOD, keep us safe from their lies, from the wicked who stalk us with lies.

PSALM 12:5–7 MSG

. . . .

God, You speak into our messes. In the dark hovels where we hide and suffer, Your words penetrate the gloom and desperation to bring light and life. You came to heal our wretched hearts. To soothe away the ache in our lives and replace it with hope in You. Hope in Your promises to care for us and give us a good future. You have plans for me. Plans that have nothing to do with disaster and depression. Instead, You orchestrate hope and goodness into my future with You. Help me to hold tightly to Your promises amid the world's lies. Because Your words are flawless, like silver refined in a crucible. It's not in Your nature to speak an untrue word. In Jesus' name, amen.

Eternity in Our Hearts

Yet God has made everything beautiful for its own time.
He has planted eternity in the human heart, but even so,
people cannot see the whole scope of God's
work from beginning to end.
ECCLESIASTES 3:11 NLT

God, so many of us try to live and move and be without You, outside of Your purpose for our life. But no matter how many pursuits we entertain, apart from You, they all come up empty. We're left with that gnawing sense that there's something more, something big, epic even, that we're missing. We feel that unfulfilled expectation in the core of our being because You created us to need You. You placed eternity in our hearts so that we could never be totally satisfied without You. Thank You, God, that You gave me that yearning for You. I have an assurance coded into the fiber of my existence that You are there and that I need You. That I was made for eternity. In Jesus' name, amen.

He's Enough

Jesus Christ is the same yesterday and today and forever.
Do not be carried away by all kinds of strange teachings.
It is good for our hearts to be strengthened by grace.
HEBREWS 13:8–9

Father, some think that Your plan is too easy—just ask and receive. They want to add more and require some further action on our part. Surely we should have to clean ourselves up a bit and try to be presentable. But they've missed the truth that we need You so desperately because we're helpless to rescue ourselves. We can't add anything to the beautiful simplicity of Your grace. Jesus was enough then, and He's enough now. His sacrifice was sufficient for my sin—all of it. I can never go so far that Your grace won't cover me. And that will never change, because You never change. Strengthen my heart with Your amazing, boundless, wonderful, and completely undeserved grace. In Jesus' name, amen.

EVEN IF. . .

Shadrach, Meshach, and Abednego replied, "O Nebuchadnezzar, we do not need to defend ourselves before you. If we are thrown into the blazing furnace, the God whom we serve is able to save us. He will rescue us from your power, Your Majesty. But even if he doesn't, we want to make it clear to you, Your Majesty, that we will never serve your gods or worship the gold statue you have set up."
DANIEL 3:16–18 NLT

God, Your ways are so much bigger than me. And yet You care about my experiences. You see every hurt and capture my tears in a bottle. You see every slight, every unkind word said to me, every unfair action against me, and You take note. You know me intimately and love me greater than anyone else loves me. I trust that You are able to redeem the harm that others intend for me and use it for Your glory. You are powerful enough to deliver me from whatever blazing furnace I find myself in, but I know that even if You don't, there's more than this life waiting for me on the other side. Show me the breathtaking maturity You envision for me out of the ashes of my struggles. Amen.

LIVING THE GOOD LIFE

And remember that the heavenly Father to whom you pray has no favorites. He will judge or reward you according to what you do. So you must live in reverent fear of him during your time here as "temporary residents." For you know that God paid a ransom to save you from the empty life you inherited from your ancestors. And it was not paid with mere gold or silver, which lose their value. It was the precious blood of Christ.

1 PETER 1:17–19 NLT

Heavenly Father, You ransomed me from an empty life through the precious blood of Your Son, Jesus. I owe You big time for Your extravagant grace. My debt to You is unfathomable. But You didn't buy me from death to enslave me. You paid my price out of pure love. Because of that I serve You for the sheer joy of pleasing You. You reward Your faithful followers in this temporary life. When I am beat down from the struggle, remind me that this life is a pin prick in time. But what I do with this speck of time will impact my eternity. I long to hear "Well done, My good and faithful child" when I see You face-to-face. Amen.

BATTLE TRAINING

*Praise the LORD, who is my rock. He trains my hands for war
and gives my fingers skill for battle. He is my loving ally
and my fortress, my tower of safety, my rescuer.
He is my shield, and I take refuge in him.*
PSALM 144:1–2 NLT

God, You know that following You positions me in direct conflict
with Your enemy, Satan. This earth is a war-torn battlefield of souls,
and I'm living in desperate times. But You are the Master Instructor.
I'm not left defenseless, because You train me to fight and give me
the skills I need to be an over-comer. Lord, school me in holy living
so I can shelter in You, my Rock. Instruct me to effectively wield my
spiritual armor. Teach me to skillfully slash through the enemy's
lies with the sword of the Spirit, Your Word, and to defend well
against flaming arrows of fear and doubt with the broad shield of
my faith in You. Teach me to trust and obey to win the day. Amen.

Rest in His Strength

His pleasure is not in the strength of the horse, nor his delight
in the legs of the warrior; the LORD delights in those who
fear him, who put their hope in his unfailing love.

PSALM 147:10–11

Lord, I've tried doing things in my own strength. I've trusted in my own plans, my own initiative, and allowed my pride to guide me into thinking that I've accomplished my goals with no one to thank but myself. Forgive me, Father, for putting my trust in the wrong place and for my arrogance in believing I am the great mover and shaker who makes things happen in my life. Teach me to rely on and wait for You. I've made a mess of things in the past because I was impatient. Instead of seeking Your will, I rushed forward to do something, anything, not to feel helpless. But my true hope rests in Your love that never fails. In Jesus' name, amen.

A Better Place

All these people were still living by faith when they died. They did not receive the things promised; they only saw them and welcomed them from a distance, admitting that they were foreigners and strangers on earth. People who say such things show that they are looking for a country of their own. . . . They were longing for a better country—a heavenly one. Therefore God is not ashamed to be called their God, for he has prepared a city for them.

Hebrews 11:13–14, 16

God, don't let me get too comfortable here. This world is not my final home. This place is fraught with sin and death and disease. Hardships and incomprehensible evil too often rule here. But I have hope of a better place. A place of wonders and light. I can see it in the distance and I'm waiting eagerly for the time when I can join You there. Like a parent excited to see their child's joy on Christmas morning, I know that You're giddy with anticipation to show us, Your children, the amazing and unbelievable home You are preparing for us in heaven. Give me an eternal focus as I try to live my life with the promise of an unimaginably good future ever before me. Amen.

Giant Slayer

*David said to the Philistine, "You come against me with sword and spear and javelin, but I come against you in the name of the L*ORD *Almighty, the God of the armies of Israel, whom you have defied. This day the L*ORD *will deliver you into my hands. . .and the whole world will know that there is a God in Israel."*

1 SAMUEL 17:45–46

God, giants still plunder our lands. We battle the giants of anxiety, depression, selfishness, pride, and anger. They scoff at us just as Goliath laughed at David for standing before him with five stones. But thank You, God, You are still in the business of defeating mammoth enemies. When I come up against big problems in this world, I will stand bravely before them and say, "I come against you in the name of the Lord Almighty." May others see my faith in You and Your care for me and recognize that there is a mighty God of the universe. Use me to draw others to You. Give me courage and patience to wait on You because You have promised to fight for me. In Jesus' name, amen.

KINSMAN-REDEEMER

"May the LORD repay you for what you have done.
May you be richly rewarded by the LORD, the God of Israel,
under whose wings you have come to take refuge."
RUTH 2:12

. . . .

God, You have chosen the poor of this world—the poor in spirit, the oppressed, and the vulnerable. Ruth, a virtuous woman but also a destitute widow, found kindness and protection in Boaz, who foreshadows another kindhearted kinsman-redeemer—Jesus! Through His act of redemption, Jesus takes His bride, the church. He was born in human form to share in our weakness and bloodline, and through His perfect obedience was able to redeem us. He willingly laid down His life on the cross. Jesus, thank You for Your willingness to redeem us, to buy us back and provide us with a future. Thank You for Your love and abundant kindness. In the name of Jesus, amen.

My Future Joy

Let us run with endurance the race God has set before us. We do this by keeping our eyes on Jesus, the champion who initiates and perfects our faith. Because of the joy awaiting him, he endured the cross, disregarding its shame. Now he is seated in the place of honor beside God's throne. Think of all the hostility he endured from sinful people; then you won't become weary and give up.

HEBREWS 12:1–3 NLT

Heavenly Father, words can't even express my gratitude for Jesus. Not only has He saved me from a horrible fate and given me the opportunity to have a relationship with You, but He is my perfect example, my encouragement to keep going, to never give up when I'm tired. At times, I look around and wonder why I'm striving to do the right thing. Why I'm working so hard to follow You in a corrupt world when it seems like everyone who simply lives for themselves is getting so much more out of life than I am. But then I remember Jesus. He endured more than I ever will for the joy awaiting Him in eternity. And because He did, I can persevere for the promise. Amen.

Never Too Far

*And God raised us up with Christ. . .in order that in the coming ages
he might show the incomparable riches of his grace, expressed in his
kindness to us in Christ Jesus. For it is by grace you have been saved,
through faith—and this is not from yourselves, it is the gift of
God—not by works, so that no one can boast.*

<small>Ephesians 2:6–9</small>

God, I can never outrun Your grace or reach the border of Your
mercy. Just when I think I've gone too far, reached a limit where
Your grace cannot extend, I find Your love and mercy there too. No
matter what I've done, no matter how dirty Satan tries to convince
me I've become, You can raise me to new life in Christ and wash
clean my stains. Because it's not about the things that I've done,
it's about who You are as the merciful God of heaven and earth.
You've gifted me with extravagant grace I could never afford. My
feeble attempts to please You could never purchase such a price-
less treasure. Yet You give it away freely. In Jesus' name, amen.

LORD OF PEACE

Now may the Lord of peace himself give you his peace at all times and in every situation. The Lord be with you all.

2 THESSALONIANS 3:16 NLT

Lord, our world is teeming with anxiety disorders and fears. We suffer in a prison of stress we've built around ourselves. Our minds need rest that can come only from You, the Lord of peace. Free my mind from worry and teach me to trust fully in You. Flood my mind with Your peace at all times and in every situation I encounter. Make my confidence: "If God is for me who can be against me? What can mere man do to me?" (Romans 8:31). Because You are for me, God. I am Yours, chosen before time to be Your daughter. Grant me peace of mind and soul in turbulent times so others will be drawn to Your love through me. In Jesus' name, amen.

I Am Accepted

"Those the Father has given me will come to me, and I will never reject them. For I have come down from heaven to do the will of God who sent me, not to do my own will. And this is the will of God, that I should not lose even one of all those he has given me, but that I should raise them up at the last day."

JOHN 6:37–39 NLT

. . . .

Father in heaven, I don't have to hide my flaws and failures or clean myself up to come to You. I can come as I am with no fear that You will reject me, because You came for the humble at heart. I've been cast aside by others, and it hurts. Their callous indifference threatened to strip me of my worth. But then I heard Your voice. You said, "Come." And Your forgiveness is available to anyone who asks. Your infinite grace covers all. You love me and welcome me because You created me. As a loving Father, You fold me in Your arms. When You return, You will raise me to new life with a glorious new resurrection body. In Jesus' name, amen.

The Day Is Near

And do this, understanding the present time: The hour has already come for you to wake up from your slumber, because our salvation is nearer now than when we first believed. The night is nearly over; the day is almost here. So let us put aside the deeds of darkness and put on the armor of light.

ROMANS 13:11–12

Heavenly Father, with each passing day, I'm closer to eternity. You're putting the finishing touches on the home You have built for us in heaven, and I don't want to waste a minute of the time I'm given here. Keep me from becoming distracted with my day-to-day earthly life and wake me up to what You are doing around me. I want to participate in Your good work. I want to cast off all my sin and put on Jesus. Don't allow me to be numbed by pleasure and comfort or to go grasping after everything I can get in this temporary life. Keep my eyes focused on eternity, for time is short. In the name of Jesus, amen.

He Is Near

"Starting from scratch, he made the entire human race and made the earth hospitable, with plenty of time and space for living so we could seek after God, and not just grope around in the dark but actually find him. He doesn't play hide-and-seek with us. He's not remote; he's near. We live and move in him, can't get away from him! One of your poets said it well: 'We're the God-created.'"
ACTS 17:26–28 MSG

God, I played hide-and-seek as a child. I've felt the frustration from that last person who hid so well I just can't see them anywhere. But You aren't playing games with me. You want to be found and understood and loved. You don't delight in confusion and tricks. You've given us space and time to seek You out, to find You. You don't hold Yourself back from us. You're near, right in front of me! In fact, my whole being is wrapped intrinsically in You because You are my Maker. I'm Your offspring, Your beloved daughter. I may not always know exactly what You're doing through every circumstance I encounter, but I can know the goodness of Your character and trust in Your love. Amen.

Graciously Blessed

John testified about him when he shouted to the crowds, "This is the one I was talking about when I said, 'Someone is coming after me who is far greater than I am, for he existed long before me.'" From his abundance we have all received one gracious blessing after another.
JOHN 1:15–16 NLT

God, complaining comes easier to me than recognizing the ways I have been blessed. My perspective desperately needs an overhaul. My focus is too often snagged on my problems and all the things that are less than what I desire. But I have realized that I need to adopt an attitude of thanksgiving. Because while I allow one small snag to steal my joy, I miss the blessings flooding into my life. If I breathe, I am alive, even if my health is less than perfect. I have spiritual life in You. I have hope and peace and love through Christ. I have received mercy and grace. I am rich beyond measure in You! Open my eyes to the countless blessings I've been given. Amen.

CALMED

If GOD hadn't been there for me, I never would have made it.
The minute I said, "I'm slipping, I'm falling," your love, GOD,
took hold and held me fast. When I was upset and beside
myself, you calmed me down and cheered me up.

PSALM 94:17–19 MSG

Lord, this earth is a tumultuous place. It's a frenzy of emotions and circumstances that threaten to sweep us away into upheaval. But when frantic anxiety rises within me, I look to You. You are the Good Shepherd who leads me beside still waters and restores my soul. You are the Master of creation who looks at my storm and orders, "Be still." And if You don't calm the storm surge around me, You calm my soul and bring me through rough waters. I have found lasting peace in trusting You. You comfort my fears and soothe my anxiety. No matter what befalls me in this life, I am calm in Your care. In the name of Jesus, amen.

Never Abandoned

My God, my God, why have you abandoned me? Why are you so far away when I groan for help? Every day I call to you, my God, but you do not answer. Every night I lift my voice, but I find no relief. Yet you are holy, enthroned on the praises of Israel. Our ancestors trusted in you, and you rescued them. . . . For he has not ignored or belittled the suffering of the needy.
PSALM 22:1–4, 24 NLT

. . . .

Father, You're big enough to handle my emotions. You don't shun me when I come to You with honest feelings of pain and discouragement. You don't shame me for feeling alone or abandoned or for questioning why I'm suffering. Instead You comfort me with reminders that my faith is not misplaced. You remind me of Your long story of faithfulness to those who love and trust You. You do not ignore or belittle those who are suffering. You have kept all of Your promises throughout history. You are the Holy One who is incapable of lies. Protect my mind from Satan's whispers that You have abandoned me. Give me wisdom to see Your truth and gentle love. In the name of Jesus, amen.

Thirsty for You

As the deer pants for streams of water, so my soul pants for you,
my God. My soul thirsts for God, for the living God.
When can I go and meet with God?

PSALM 42:1–2

. . . .

God, I need You. You are the quenching, sustaining water that feeds my soul. Keep my eyes from the distractions that would tear me away from my wholehearted devotion to You. My heart belongs completely to You. May my love for You never be divided among the shallow things of earth. Never allow my day-to-day life to become so consuming that I neglect to meet with You, that I miss the bigger picture of Your purpose for my life. Keep my soul thirsty for You and my desire strong to spend time with my Savior every day. I anticipate my moments and hours with You with eagerness. Like a parched desert wanderer, I crave a deeper relationship with You, the living God who gives me life. Amen.

FUTURE GLORY

I consider that our present sufferings are not worth comparing with the glory that will be revealed in us. For the creation waits in eager expectation for the children of God to be revealed.
ROMANS 8:18–19

. . . .

God, I can't wait for my future with You. Here, I struggle and suffer. But the apostle Paul said that anything that befalls me in this life is nothing but a momentary discomfort compared to the glory of eternity. Keep in the forefront of my mind the truth that this life is short and eternity is long. When I see You, I will be made new. I will be alive as I never have been before with a resurrection body. It will be me as I was always meant to be. The me that You envisioned when You created me. The best version of myself. I can't wait to behold the wonders of Your glory and embrace life eternal—millions of years and still more with You. Amen.

Jesus, Champion of My Faith

Do you see what this means—all these pioneers who blazed the way, all these veterans cheering us on? It means we'd better get on with it. Strip down, start running—and never quit! No extra spiritual fat, no parasitic sins. Keep your eyes on Jesus, who both began and finished this race we're in. Study how he did it. Because he never lost sight of where he was headed—that exhilarating finish in and with God.

Hebrews 12:1–2 MSG

Lord, I can envision it now. My days in this earthly life have ended and I'm walking up the golden streets of heaven toward Your glorious throne. Crowds swell along the road and they're cheering and celebrating—for me. I've run my race well. I followed Jesus, who showed me how to keep my eye on eternity; I've overcome and endured; and I've reached my heart-pounding finish line. Jesus steps forward and hugs me hard. He pulls back, and He's smiling wide. I'm a joint-heir with Him. My Father cups His palms around my face with kind eyes shining and says, "Well done, My daughter." Lord, make this my reality. Help me throw off sin and train me to think of eternity. Amen.

Scripture Index

Genesis
9:9–11 119

Exodus
15:2 65

Numbers
23:19 . . . . 41, 152

Deuteronomy
3:21–22 143
31:6 140

Ruth
2:12 192

1 Samuel
2:2 113
17:45–46 191

2 Chronicles
16:8–9 177

Job
8:13–15 57
8:21 48
12:7–10 169

Psalms
1:1–3 62
10:17–18 157
12:5–7 183
16:7–8 168
16:8–9, 11 156
19:1–4, 7 90
22:1–4, 24 201
23:1–3 137
23:1–4 21
27:13–14 180
32:4–5 141
34:4–5 100
34:17–19 74
37:1–4 163
37:10–11 97

37:18 176
38:12–15 28
39:4–7 11
42:1–2 202
43:4–5 19
46:1–3, 7 126
46:10–11 52
48:14 153
51:9–12 173
56:8–10 179
61:1–4 158
62:3–6 13
63:1–4 75
63:5 77
68:19–20 154
71:14–15 38
71:19–20 96
73:21–26 165
78:7–8 24
94:17–19 200
103:2–5 159
103:12 164
103:13–14 131
118:24 123
119:71–72 170
119:105 160
121:2–3 155
136:1–6 5
139:1–5 94
139:14–16 69
139:23–24 108
144:1–2 188
147:10–11 189
149:3–5 95

Proverbs
3:5–6 55
24:13–14 15

Ecclesiastes
3:11 184

Isaiah
9:7 34

26:3–4 162
30:18. 116
40:25–26 138
40:27–28 150
40:28–31 17
41:9–10. 10
43:16, 18–19 129
45:18–20, 22. 134
49:15–16 58
54:10. 167
61:1–3 130
66:13–14 110

Jeremiah
29:11–14 8
31:3 70
31:3–4 182
31:34 148
33:2–3 171

Lamentations
3:19–24. 18
3:25–26. 39
Ezekiel
36:26–28 122

Daniel
3:16–18 186

Hosea
2:13–15 78
2:14–15 12
11:9 181

Zephaniah
3:15–17 20
3:17 175

Matthew
5:3–6. 147
5:7 135
7:7–8 . . . . .45, 178
7:24–25 117
9:35–36. 149
22:31–32 166

Luke
1:31–33 26
9:23–25 79
15:22–24. 127
22:39–40 89
23:39–43. 46

John
1:1–5 16
1:14–15 111
1:15–16 199
3:16–18. 172
4:13–14 42
6:37–39 196
6:48–51. 139
10:7–10. 47
14:4–7 86
14:27. 114
15:1–4 87
15:15–17 104

Acts
2:25–28. 66
17:26–28 198

Romans
1:20. 115
4:20–24 61
5:2–5 35
8:1–3. 32
8:18–19. 203
8:23–26 6
8:26–28 22
8:37–39 84
12:9–14. 7
13:11–12. 197
15:4 109
15:12–13. 36
15:13 64

1 Corinthians
2:10–12. 33
4:19–20 144
5:6–8 136
6:9–11 107
10:13 53